# HELL NO

## BY

## Marc D. Royer Ph.D.

# Hell No

**Copyright 1999
Marc D. Royer
First Printing 1999**

Scripture quotations are taken from the New International Version Copyright 1983, Zondervan Corporation. Used by permission.

**Published by:
The Christian Resource Group
11664 Red Oak Dr.
Granger, IN 46530
(219) 273-6235**


ISBN: 0-7392-0408-4

LOC: 99-95706


Printed in the USA by

**MORRIS PUBLISHING**
3212 East Highway 30 • Kearney, NE 68847 • 1-800-650-7888

## OTHER BOOKS BY DR. MARC ROYER:

*Secrets: Exposing, Resolving, & Overcoming the Secrets We Carry With Us*

*Handling Death, Dying, and Grief*

*Rejection: Turning Your Lemons Into Lemonade*

*Happiness In 30 Days or Less*

*Financial Freedom Starting Today*

*Practical Patience*

*Building the Home of Your Dreams*

*The Development Manual Series*
*Volume I: A Study in the Old Testament*
*Volume II: A Study in the New Testament*
*A Study in the Life of David*
*A Study in the Prophets*

**Write:**
**The Christian Resource Group**
**11664 Red Oak Drive**
**Granger, Indiana 46530**

or
Request These Titles From Your Local Bookstore

# Hell No

# INTRODUCTION

I have always been fascinated with the way people use the word, "hell." I was raised to believe that the use of the word hell in language was swearing, and my opinions stem from this. I guess I must have gone through a discovery stage where I carefully contemplated how people use "hell" in conversation.

"Oh, hell yes!" "Hell no!" "That was a hell-of-a (helluva) (whatever)!" These phrases were never part of my personal vocabulary because of the image I have of the awful place. If people could become aware of the literal destination of hell, their response would be a resounding, "Hell! No way!" I shorten this response to "Hell...no!" Never again would people be comfortable using that word as slang.

Many people simply don't see hell as a literal place. There are even religious groups who downplay its existence. Some don't believe in the literal destiny of hell at all.

Jesus referred to the dimensions of hell many times more than he did heaven. The remarkable thing about this is that Jesus gave us all the necessary truths to avoid hell.

There are several concepts in Scripture concerning what is commonly referred to as hell. The basic ones are Hades, Sheol, and Gehenna. There are several interpretations of these words. There are also prophetic applications made of them. Sheol is known as the place of the dead. Gehenna was a place in Jerusalem where garbage was burned. Hades is the abode of the dead while awaiting judgment. There are many things written about these three places. It is also written that the final place of the condemned is the "lake of fire." We can put an end to the confusion if we put an emphasis on three words and their meanings:

**Hades**: This word in the Old Testament referred to where all the dead go. "Abraham's bosom" was an upper part where the righteous abode. This was also referred to as paradise. Those righteous people who lived before Christ were waiting for Him to come and take them to heaven with Him. This place was paradise, separated by an impassable gulf from lower Hades, the place of the unrighteous. This lower part was a place of torment for those people awaiting final judgment. It seems that the residents of both upper and lower Hades could see each other. Those in lower Hades constantly regretted not having lived better lives.

**Hell**: This was a newer term adopted in the New Testament to replace Hades, and now is the place of the unsaved who are awaiting judgment. Although hell is a temporary place until the Day of Judgment, it is nonetheless a miserable place of torture and torment. The saved are in heaven.

**Lake of Fire**: This place replaces hell. Death, hell, and all of those whose name is not written in the Book of Life are cast into the lake of fire. It seems that the lake of fire has two interesting qualities different from Hades or hell:

1.  The lake of fire is a place of considerable and greatly intense misery.

2.  The lake of fire continues without end or relief through all eternity.

The prophets, the psalmist, Jonah — even Jesus — referred to hell-like abodes. Many of these references appear to be inferences of current feelings or states rather than an eternal state.

# CHAPTER 1

## "GOING LIKE A BAT OUT OF HELL"

I was five years old when the reality of hell fully gripped me. My brothers and I were at my grandparents' farm during summer vacation. August 5 is my birthday and I was presented a very special birthday present — **a new swimming pool**. It was a new variety. The flexible side vinyl liner, two-foot pools had just come out and Grandma had bought one for me. It was with great excitement that Grandma set it up and we began to fill it with water from the well. We were experiencing a summer drought and Grandpa made it clear that he was opposed to using the well water for something as silly as a swimming pool when the cows needed the water more. Further, he would mutter about the creek down by the culvert being good enough for him to swim in and it should be good enough for us, too.

Nevertheless, Grandma always won out; partially because she never paid much attention to what others said, and partially because of how much she loved her grandsons.

It took all day to fill that little two-foot pool because the cows kept coming up for a drink and the well pump could only work so hard.

After it was full, we had to wait the rest of the afternoon until the sun could heat the pool water up. In the Midwest, water takes a long time to heat up. It usually takes Lake Michigan until Labor Day to actually feel comfortable.

All afternoon we waited for Grandma's permission to get in the pool. Every 15 minutes we would ask Grandma if we could get in, only to be turned down. My grandparents raised their niece Glenda from childhood. She was 15 years older than we were, and was like an aunt to us. All day long she could hear us hounding Grandma to let us get into that pool. Finally during chore time Grandma gave in — as long as we took off our shoes and socks, and only waded in the pool. Off we went. In the pool we squealed and yelled and carried on. It wasn't long before Glenda came to her bedroom window and yelled at us. "Who told you boys you could get in the pool!" she demanded.

"Grandma did."

"Are you lying to me, Marc?" she asked.

"No," I replied.

Then she said something with such great conviction it has been etched on my soul ever since. "Marc, do you know where liars go?"

I was puzzled because I didn't know what in the world she could mean. "No," I replied.

"Come on," she said, "Of course you know where liars go!"

"No, I don't know where liars go!" I yelled.

"They go down," she said while pointing downward.

"Down?" I inquired. I was really puzzled.

"Yes, down. Down to where the devil is."

Now I was really getting scared. But I repeated out loud exactly what she had said — "Down to where the devil is?"

"Hell!" She said.

"Hell?" I questioned.

"Yes, hell!" she exclaimed, very frustrated that I wasn't catching on to this concept that I should have already known about.

Right at this point my grandmother broke in. Glenda apparently saw her coming, which is why she seemed in such a frustrated hurry to get the upstairs window down from where she was yelling.

"What in the world is all the swearing about?" my grandmother demanded.

"Oh never mind!" Glenda said curtly, "This dumb kid doesn't know anything about the devil or hell and he won't try to listen."

Just before the window was completely down I heard her grunt, "To hell with him!"

That night my grandmother spent several hours talking about what hell was and showing me Scriptures. It was the most unusual day of my life. It left an indelible impression upon me. But then, hell as a definite place, is worthy of leaving a lasting impression! Coming face to face with the awful reality of such a place is as essential as coming face to face with the reality of a savior. Coming face to face with the knowledge that there is a heaven to gain and a hell to shun is the most basic information in the journey of faith. It is to this place we all must come.

The challenge to face the fact that there exists eternalness after this present temporalness is a great debate that has fueled philosophical discussions for centuries. Whether or not one chooses to believe or not believe seems to be less important than the fact that so many have never been challenged to think about it. Lest we think this is overstated, we must ask ourselves: How many people have I challenged recently with the thought of eternity?

Luke 16:19-31 provides us with a well-known story commonly known as, "The Rich Man and Lazarus." This story brings to light the awful reality of a literal hell. It is simply not a story we can avoid. Within its context we can develop some very real concepts about the realities associated with the notion of hell. Some of these may seem quite elementary — others quite simple. But, when dealing with such a consuming subject, we don't dare take any chance of omission. We must see and understand Jesus' own story. His purpose was to fully impact each of us with the awful reality of hell and thereby cause us to make our own decisions of destiny.

*"There was a rich man who was dressed in purple and fine linen and lived in luxury every day. At his gate was laid a beggar named Lazarus, covered with sores and longing to eat what fell from the rich man's table. Even the dogs came and licked his sores. The time came when the beggar died and the angels carried him to Abraham's side. The rich man also died and was buried. In hell, where he was in torment, he looked up and saw Abraham far away, with Lazarus by his side. So he called to him, 'Father Abraham, have pity on me and send Lazarus to dip the tip of his finger in water and cool my tongue, because I am in agony in this fire.' But Abraham replied, 'Son, remember that in your lifetime you received your good things, while Lazarus received bad things, but now he is comforted here and you are in agony. And besides all this, between us and you a great chasm has been fixed, so that those who want to go from here to you cannot, nor can anyone cross over from there to us.' He answered, 'Then I beg you, father, send Lazarus to my father's house, for I have five brothers. Let him warn them, so that they will not also come to this place of torment.' Abraham replied, 'They have Moses and the Prophets; let them listen to them.' 'No, father Abraham,' he said, 'but if someone from the dead goes to them, they will repent.' He said to him, 'If they do not listen to Moses and the Prophets, they will not be convinced even if someone rises from the dead.'"* — *Luke 16:19-31*

**Reality #1: The Physical Condition in Life Does Not Reflect the Internal Condition of the Soul. v. 19**

Judging on the outward appearance seems to be an inherent part of our humanness. We continue to do this despite the real evidence. The evidence proves we cannot develop any patterns of behavior verses guaranteeing success. Many speakers, including preachers, have tried to show us that Christians will always be prosperous. Whenever we use the word <u>always</u> when referring to God, we <u>always</u> get into trouble. The ground we stand on is often shaky.

There are just too many variables to be able to say this person or that person is blessed for this or that reason. This has been a great debate for centuries. The Book of Job was written in an attempt to delve deeply into this question. The answer comes from the Gospels — "He causes his sun to rise on the evil and the good."

When Christians say that God has blessed "me" because of my righteous life; they are really making a broader statement than they dare make — or at least more than they should. The idea that God has blessed "me" because "I am righteous" leaves an open end to those who are not prosperous. There are, in fact, both rich and poor righteous people. There are also rich and poor unrighteous people. The bottom line is we should not draw a conclusion concerning another person's spiritual condition based upon his material possessions.

We already know that our "rich man" in the story was dressed in purple and fine linen, which was the most expensive dress in that culture. It is interesting to realize that in the culture of the day, if you had money it was obvious by your dress.

In some cultures, like Australia, the rich folk dress badly. They are obvious in their poorly coordinated colors.

Nevertheless, every culture has its status symbols and places of decadence.

The rich man in the text was wealthy with no soul. The poor man was poverty stricken, but wealthy in spirit. We cannot judge the internal by the external.

## Reality #2: What We Do to Help Hurting People Reflects the Condition of Our Soul. v. 20

Early in this story we are brought to a powerful paradox. Just outside this rich man's home lay a beggar covered with sores. This is one of the greatest contrasts you will ever find between luxury and poverty. Since the poor man actually lay at the gate of the rich man's estate, it further gives us an insight into the rich man's heart. Because this was an ongoing condition, clearly the rich man had ignored the beggar's pleading.

Reaching out to help someone in need should not be something that requires dialogue or careful debate. To reach out to hurting people is indeed a reflection of the heart. We could take it much further and say that our acts of benevolence actually reveal the condition of our souls.

The dog is a despicable creature in eastern culture. To live with dogs as the text ascribes is to have insult added to injury. The real indictment is toward the rich man. Because this was the very gate he came through, he chose to ignore this sick beggar.

Works alone do not redeem us. Good deeds are important, but they will not stand on their own. The truth is benevolence may not be an end in itself, but it is certainly a means to an end by revealing to us the condition of the soul.

The rich man probably had every excuse to ignore the poor man. Maybe he was in a hurry. He perhaps had other appointments. It might be he thought this beggar was lazy and didn't want to work. Maybe his upbringing did not allow him to associate with the less fortunate.

Whatever the reason or excuse, he ignored this poor beggar in need. There are many excuses to use to avoid those in need, but keep in mind, they are all a reflection of one's soul.

### Reality #3: Coping with the Many Developments Which Life Brings Creates Depth Within the Soul. v. 21

The sick beggar Lazarus stayed at the rich man's gate with great hope of getting scraps that were thrown out with the garbage. It is a gruesome picture portrayed — a pauper sick with sores living with the dogs that licked his sores and fed off his flesh. With this continual irritation, his sores could never heal. He was at the bottom — flat on his back looking up. His only consolation in life was to be fortunate enough to find a scrap of edible food in the garbage.

People who live this way have it tough. There are many different needs and cares and burdens. But people are the same; each one trying to make the best out of his life that he can. (Some make out better than others.)

An important point needs to be made here: Lazarus was not righteous because he was poor, but because of what his affliction brought about within his soul. Being able to take one's afflictions and difficulties and use them to become a better person is the whole purpose of a harder life.

If it is true that the good life tends to make one soft, then those who are able to take hard times and become stronger really come out ahead by having less. Whether this is or is not always true is scrutinized in every life. The reality is that we should not be afraid of the hard times. They can become our link to a better internal life if we let them. We should not look down upon those less fortunate, for they may actually be the most spiritually strong. Whatever develops in one's life can be handled.  Further, if we allow it, we may become better people by becoming deeper within the soul.

Allow your afflictions to create righteousness like Lazarus did.

### Reality #4: There is a Definite Conscious Level Beyond this Present Life. v. 22-23

When I was in the ninth grade, I remember an interesting conversation with my assistant wrestling coach.  Coach Davidson was in charge of our conditioning.  He was the head coach of our undefeated football team, but he didn't know anything about wrestling.

Because he didn't know much about the technical aspects of wrestling, our head coach wanted him to work out with us. Because we were about the same weight, he was usually my partner.  He was quite strong, but didn't know the moves or the strategy and I always got the best of him.  One time he got lucky and reversed a hold.  At that point he said something kind of cute: "Prepare to meet your maker!"  I quickly reversed his advantage and buried my chin in the middle of his back.  I then asked him a point blank question: "Do you believe in heaven and hell?"  He replied interestingly, "I believe in some form of life after death." We didn't have the time to discuss it further, after all this was a fast-moving wrestling practice.  Besides, the coach was getting concerned about our lack of attentiveness.

Coach Davidson verbalized a very common feeling.  Many believe in some form of the great beyond, but can't rightly spell out what is the form of life they propose.  This mentality is lacking.  We must develop a view of the beyond to help us live out a more meaningful existence here and now.

**Reality #5: There are Two Divisions in the Next Life. One is Paradise, the other is an Agony of Fire. v. 24**

The text spells out two very essential forms of existence — the first, paradise, and the second a place of torment. A belief system that includes these two points is essential. That there really is a heaven to gain and a hell to shun is the one very critical key to keep our behavior in check, both as an individual and as a society. The belief in heaven and hell actually helps us all!

This reality continues on from the last reality. Not only must we establish a life hereafter, but also we must establish a consciousness of what kind of life. In the text we see that the roles of Lazarus and the rich man are reversed. The "why" and "wherefore" of this will be looked at later, but the central focus here is what the eternal destinies are. Clearly one man is being comforted in the presence of Abraham, while the other is in agony, which is even described as "fire."

Whether one interprets this literally or figuratively, the scene still remains quite vivid. Both men have a very conscious presence. They are quite aware of what their destinies mean. They feel, think, perceive and reflect. The difference between the two is striking: one is in paradise, the other in the agony of fire.

A very obvious fact from the story that is different from the belief system of many worshippers is that there are no other options. There is no in between. There is no purgatory.

Jesus told this story on purpose. This was His scenario. This fifth reality is a central focus of the great storyteller Himself. Jesus intends for us to fully realize that our eternal destinies are within only a two-option course.

Risking sounding too "preachy," it behooves us to develop a belief system that accommodates this idea.

## Reality #6: Evaluation on a Daily Basis Provides the Key to Stay on Course. v. 25

The rich man is at such a conscious level that he has plenty of time to think. In the text of the story, the rich man asks for some help from Abraham. Abraham diverts his thinking back to his life.

Eternity will be an everlasting time of thinking. Thinking back upon time after time when you erred — times when things could have been different — times of selfishness, greed, pride, deceit, and on and on. This eternal evaluation could honestly be hell all in itself — without the "agony of fire."

It simply does not have to come to this. We don't have to end this life and then go on to eternal regret and evaluation. The way to avoid this is to determine to evaluate your life on a daily basis. Daily self-evaluation on a critical scale helps keep one on course. The course one keeps on will lead to paradise, not to the agony of fire. Keeping current on your own behavior will truly keep you on the narrow path.

## Reality #7: The Destiny of Eternal Life is Determined in this Life and Cannot be Changed in the Next. v. 26

Abraham tells the rich man in the story, that there was a great chasm that had been fixed. There was no crossing over.

Do we determine our destiny in this life, but once eternity has been set into motion, there is no changing it?

The awful reality is that no matter how hard it sounds, the things we do today determine our destiny tomorrow. The way to keep this in perspective is to realize that we must not trade something eternal for something temporal. It is simply not wise to serve the flesh when it is so temporary. The way of strength is to be so convinced of this truth that it guides all of our activities.

Developing discipline can be one's greatest asset in this age of moral decay. Being reminded of our eternal destiny must be brought down to a more practical day-to-day level of developing boundaries in lifestyle, as well as the implementation of personal convictions.

Any feeling of loss, any sensation of pain, any self-deprivation is strictly temporary. Eternal paradise is worth any temporary sacrifice.

**Reality #8: All that is Necessary to Reach Eternal Paradise is Simple Obedience to God's Word. v. 27-29**

All that is necessary to achieve eternal life and to avoid the "agony of fire" is to obey God's word. The inference Jesus makes is "Moses and the prophets." This is the equivalent to the Bible. Abraham, as the story goes, told the rich man that all the information his brothers needed is in God's word.

An interesting, yet penetrating truth about God's word is that it is a person's responsibility to know what God has to say. There is a ruling in IRS tax evasion cases. It is a blanket ruling that applies to anyone who tries to cop out by saying they didn't know the tax law. The ruling is: "Ignorance of the law is not a reasonable excuse." The rich man knew his brothers paid no attention to Moses and the prophets. He knew they would never believe God's word, but they would be held accountable for it anyway.

The same is true for each of us regarding the truth of God's Word in our lives. We are responsible for everything the Scripture says. Whether we study it or know it or not - we are still held accountable for the truth. Ignorance is no excuse.

The world needs to take this truth very seriously. At this point we have everything to our advantage: a free country, freedom of worship and expression, plenty of Scripture, and the convicting power of the Holy Spirit.

There is no excuse. But there will surely be many excuses, only it will be too late. Don't be caught undone or ignorant!

### Reality #9: Faith is the Essential Ingredient to Eternal Life (No Physical Evidence is Ever Enough) v. 30-31

Simply put, faith is to believe in something that you cannot actually see. Abraham tells the rich man that his brothers will never be convinced of an eternal destiny even if the dead were to come back. Faith is the essential quality of anything that is spiritual. The reason is simple: no physical evidence is ever enough to convince one whether to actually believe or not believe.

Faith is an individual thing. That is the way God intends. God wants us to believe in Him because we want to believe. He wants us to love Him because we want to love Him. He wants us to serve Him because we want to serve Him, and so forth. Faith is the link between free will and our own prescribed belief system. It is the essential element that bridges the temporal to the eternal. It is only by faith and through faith and because of faith that we may inherit eternal life.

## THE NINE REALITIES OF HELL

There are many more realities of hell than just nine. These nine are just a start. It is from here we are able to proceed into deeper and more complex answers about hell and its meanings.

As basic as many would say Jesus' story is, it is an important beginning. Often we have assumed too much in relationship to people's belief systems. It is amazing how many don't face up to the realities of our eternal state. We must maintain our ability to present and proclaim our destiny and future. Don't stop now!

# CHAPTER 2

# "ALL HELL BROKE LOOSE"

## (Interpretations of Hell)

The most important thing about hell is to make sure it is within one's personal belief system. In later chapters we will look at many different aspects of hell. An especially insightful study will be the dimensions of hell in our present lives. It is also important to look at some Biblical interpretations of hell. The original text presents us with several looks at this intriguing place that is also seen as a condition.

Hell is the word used in the King James Version of the Old Testament to translate the Hebrew word "Sheol" which signifies an "unseen state." (De. 32:22; 2 Sam. 22:6; Job 11:8; 26:6; Ps. 9:17; 16:10; 18:5; 55:15; 86:13; 116:3; 139:8; 28:15; 57:9; Ez. 31:16; 32:21; Amos 9:2; Jonah 2:2; Hab. 2:5)

The idea of an unseen state was especially prevalent in ancient civilizations. Each had their own rendition of the "other life" as well as whatever god or gods would oversee that state of being. Rarely in any civilization do we see that the unseen world was prohibited. Generally the opposite was true — the talk and dialogue about the unseen state was especially prevalent in all civilizations.

The translation of the Greek word "Hades" in the New Testament of the King James Version is also "unseen world." (Mt. 11:23; 16:18; Luke 10:15; 16:23; Acts 2:27; Rev. 1:18; 6:8; 20:13-14) Other than the religious sect of the Sadducees, most people of the oriental Near East believed in a life after death.

The Hebrews were especially credited with an even deeper version of the "unseen world" with a differential between various types of after-life treatment.

The Greek word "Gehenna" for instance is interpreted as a "significant place of torment." This place of torment as Sheol refers, is significantly more intense than Hades appears. Some religious groups say that "Gehenna" was a garbage dump in Jerusalem where trash was burned and destroyed. This concept is likely true. The problem is, some go on to develop a belief system which ties the Gehenna idea with the "Lake of Fire" concept in Revelation chapter 20. The result of this line of thought is that whole denominations believe that the sinners (unsaved) will certainly be cast into Gehenna (hell), but will vaporize and perish, never to be seen again, just like we see at the trash pile that burns at Gehenna in Jerusalem.

In developing this belief system, there is a major error: too much is made of the legalistic power of a word rather than the idea it represents. We try through word and thought to communicate things of eternal value. As best we try, we are working at a great disadvantage. The human personality and thought processes are greatly limited. Creating a logical progression of thoughts to develop a doctrine is hard work. We must be careful not to take this work too seriously, however. In all of our hard work, this is our greatest error. We take our thoughts about hell too seriously. When we do, we hurt people.

Take, for instance, the several million people who belong to the belief system which advocates those cast into the lake of fire will vaporize immediately and not be caught in an eternal punishment of everlasting torment. Their doctrine is implicitly logical and legalistic, but could be entirely wrong if any of their concepts are in error. In other words, the risk is too high to take one word so seriously. Instead, we must look at all of the evidence to conceptualize our belief systems.

The word Gehenna is not the most intense "Hades-like" word. The Greek word "tartarus" as seen in II Peter 2:4 means the "infernal region." This refers to the place where He put the angels who fell from grace. The concept is actually "to be chained in a dangerous, fiery dungeon."

There are some references where a word like Sheol is translated "grave." These references help us to expand our study of hell into that "feeling" or emotion of hell-like suffering in the human dynamic. (Gen. 37:35, 42:38, 44:29; I Sam. 2:6; I Kings 2:6; Job 7:9, 14:13, 17:13, 21:13, 24:19; Ps. 6:5, 30:3, 31:17, 29:14, 88:3, 89:48, 141:7; Prov. 1:12, 30:16; Ec. 9:10, Song of Sol. 8:6; Isa. 14:11, 38:10; Eze. 31:15, Hos. 13:14) "Pit" is seen in Num. 16:30, 33 and Job 17:16.

In the English versions, the revisers insert the Hebrew word Sheol in places where hell, grave, and pit are used. The American revisers invariably use Sheol in the American text where it occurs in the original text.

Recently, someone gave me an article that had been circulating. As the story goes, some engineers were drilling in the USSR and had gone down around nine miles. At that point they found a hell-like molten rock with hollow spaces. They heard noises like screams. After recording and re-examining the recordings, it was deduced that these were screams of millions of people. This story has been widely spread for years. It is interesting to note that it is Christian groups who tend to propagate these stories within their own groups. It seems like we spend our time verifying things we were supposed to already believe in. Then we propagate this information to others who are supposed to believe in the same thing anyway.

The point is — whatever or however you interpret the word "hell", make sure that the propagation of your belief system to others points them to Jesus Christ. The whole point of hell is not to just avoid hell, but to enjoy Jesus. **Don't miss this point, or you might not miss hell!**

# CHAPTER 3

## "HELL NO"

### (A Look at Immortality)

The truth is, the Biblical concept of immortality is <u>not simply</u> the survival of the soul after bodily death. Rather, it is the self-conscious continuance of the whole person – body and soul together. The redemption of Christ and the possession of eternal life make all this possible. The interesting and powerful truth is the Bible does not attempt to prove this doctrine. It is also true that everywhere in Scripture this undisputed postulate is assumed. The condition of the believer in this state of immortality is not some sort of boring eternal existence, but a communion with God in eternal fulfillment and satisfaction.

Even Jesus didn't feel compelled to have to prove such a thing as immortality. The times he mentioned eternity, he even appeared surprised there was any question concerning immortality.

There are many Scriptures that allude to immortality as in Nehemiah 9:5 –

> "Stand up and bless the Lord your God <u>forever and ever</u>: and blessed be thy glorious name that is exalted above all blessing and praise."

The fifteenth chapter of I Corinthians is commonly known as the resurrection chapter. It is here we develop many of our concepts about immortality.

> "But if it is preached that Christ has been raised from the dead, how can some of you say that there is no resurrection of the dead? If there is no resurrection of the dead, then not even Christ has been raised . And if Christ has not been raised, our preaching is useless

*and so is your faith. More than that, we are then found to be false witnesses about God, for we have testified about God that he raised Christ from the dead. But he did not raise him if in fact the dead are not raised. For if the dead are not raised, then Christ has not been raised either . And if Christ has not been raised, your faith is futile; you are still in your sins. Then those also who have fallen asleep in Christ are lost. If only for this life we have hope in Christ, we are to be pitied more than all men. But Christ has indeed been raised from the dead, the firstfruits of those who have fallen asleep. For since death came through a man, the resurrection of the dead comes also through a man. For as in Adam all die, so in Christ all will be made alive. But each in his own turn: Christ, the firstfruits; then, when he comes, those who belong to him. Then the end will come, when he hands over the kingdom to God the Father after he has destroyed all dominion, authority and power. For he must reign until he has put all his enemies under his feet. The last enemy to be destroyed is death. For he 'has put everything under his feet.' Now when it says that 'everything' has been put under him, it is clear that this does not include God himself, who put everything under Christ. When he has done this, then the Son himself will be made subject to him who put everything under him, so that God may be all in all. Now if there is no resurrection, what will those do who are baptized for the dead? If the dead are not raised at all, why are people baptized for them? And as for us, why do we endanger ourselves every hour? I die every day — I mean that, brothers — just as surely as I glory over you in Christ Jesus our Lord. If I fought wild beasts in Ephesus for merely human reasons, what have I gained? If the dead are not raised, "Let us eat and drink, for tomorrow we die." Do not be misled: "Bad company* corrupts good character." *Come back to your senses as you ought, and stop sinning; for there are some who are ignorant of God — I say this to your shame. But someone may ask, 'How are the dead raised? With what kind of body will they come?' How foolish! What you sow does not come to life unless it dies. When you sow, you do not plant the body that will be, but just a seed, perhaps of wheat or of something else. But God gives it a body as he has determined, and to each kind of seed he gives its own body. All flesh is not the same: Men have one kind of flesh, animals have another, birds another and fish another. There are also heavenly bodies and there are earthly bodies; but the splendor of the heavenly bodies is one kind, and the splendor of the earthly bodies is another. The sun has one kind of splendor, the moon another and the stars another; and star differs from star in splendor. So will it be with the resurrection of the dead. The body that is sown is perishable, it is raised imperishable; it is sown in dishonor, it is raised in glory; it is sown in weakness, it is raised in power; it is sown a natural body, it is raised a spiritual body. If there is a natural body, there is also a spiritual body. So it is written: "The first man Adam became a living being"; the last Adam, a life-giving spirit. The spiritual did not come first, but the natural, and after that the spiritual. The first man was of the dust of the earth, the second man from heaven. As was the earthly man, so are those who are of the earth; and as is the man from heaven, so also are those who are of heaven. And just as we have borne the likeness of the earthly man, so shall we bear the likeness of the man from heaven. I declare to you, brothers, that flesh and blood cannot inherit the kingdom of God, nor does the perishable inherit the imperishable. Listen, I tell you a mystery: We will not all sleep, but we will all be changed — in a flash, in the twinkling of an eye, at the last trumpet. For the trumpet will sound, the dead will be raised imperishable, and we will be changed. For the perishable must clothe itself with the imperishable, and the mortal with immortality. When the perishable has been clothed with the imperishable, and the mortal with immortality, then the saying that is written will come true: "Death has been swallowed up in victory."*

*"Where, O death, is your victory? Where, O death, is your sting?" — 1 Corinthians 15:12-55*

There are several things worth noting from this passage that develop our concepts concerning the mortal/immortality transition.

First, **we shall not sleep**. The idea of eternal soul sleep is not new but has been around for centuries. It is commonly held among non-believers that after this life there is nothingness. Without realizing it, these people believe in soul sleeping. The Apostle clearly decries this belief.

Secondly, **we shall be changed**. Somehow the eternal composition of our bodies will be undeniably changed from our mortal destructible body.

Thirdly, **this change will take place in a moment.** The transition from mortal to immortal will occur in a split second. Those who are already dead will be raised and resurrected, and those already alive will be changed from what they are at present. It is not really dead people made alive again as depicted in horror movies, but rather everyone will be changed into a new, and as yet unseen, life form.

Fourth, **there will be a definite moment in time when time will be no more.** When mortal becomes immortal, it will be marked with a trumpet sound. It seems that time was an actual invention to bring life to this point.

Fifth, **life cycles as we know them will be no more.** Death will be no more. Time will be gone. At this point the whole purpose of redemption will be accomplished.

Many have interpreted this passage in light of the eschatology of Revelation. Whether it is or is not the actual Second Coming is not the point of this study. The most important aspect of the passage is the fact that it gives us glimpses of the state of immortality we will all someday discover. (There is a scripture we will look at later that has the Second Coming as a direct reference.)

## THE BRIDGE TO IMMORTALITY

Years ago Bill Bright had a great youth rally that was called "Expo 72." This was a bright spot for Campus Crusade for Christ. During this time, there was a great harvest of souls. Many were led to Christ through a very simple pamphlet called "The Four Spiritual Laws." One of these powerful points showed that sinful mankind cannot reach Holy God on his own. He, in fact, needs a bridge. The bridge, as the pamphlet shows, is Jesus Christ. The great thing we can show people is that they cannot achieve immortality on their own. The greatest misnomer is that if we do more good things than bad things, we will go to heaven.

The Garden of Eden shows us that through the disobedience of our first parents, sin was introduced into the world. Its only defeat comes through the work of Jesus on the cross and our adaptation of that work into our lives.

I Thessalonians 4:13-18 clearly points out that immortality is received. It is not forced upon us, nor innately inherited. It is received, as we believe that Jesus Christ died and rose again.

*"Brothers, we do not want you to be ignorant about those who fall asleep, or to grieve like the rest of men,*

*who have no hope. We believe that Jesus died and rose again and so we believe that God will bring with Jesus those who have fallen asleep in him. According to the Lord's own word, we tell you that we who are still alive, who are left till the coming of the Lord, will certainly not precede those who have fallen asleep. For the Lord himself will come down from heaven, with a loud command, with the voice of the archangel and with the trumpet call of God, and the dead in Christ will rise first. After that, we who are still alive and are left will be caught up together with them in the clouds to meet the Lord in the air. And so we will be with the Lord forever. Therefore encourage each other with these words."* — *1 Thessalonians 4:13-18*

Further, this "believing" is more than just head knowledge. It must be exemplified in one's life through action, attitude and conduct.

*"That you may know that you have eternal life, and you may <u>believe</u> on the <u>name of the Son of God</u>."* — *I John 5:13*

Believing on "his name" is not as difficult as it may seem on the outset. Speaking in terms of someone's name means his or her character or soul. We call a believer in Christ a Christian. The actual definition of "Christian" means "Christ like." Being a Christian is more than just a one-time thing.

Romans 2:7 puts it this way:

*"To those who by persistence in doing good seek glory, honor and immortality, he will give eternal life."* — *Romans 2:7*

The best way for the believer to experience the real fullness of God in the Christian life is to experience immortality as a gift from God through Jesus.

*"But now that you have been set free from sin and have become slaves to God, the benefit you reap leads to holiness, and the result is eternal life. For the wages of sin is death, but the gift of God is eternal life in Christ Jesus our Lord."* — Romans 6:22-23

There is such a contrast between sin and eternal life. It is like darkness versus light. This contrast helps us close the ranks between what we are and what we ought to be. The choice is simple. Accept Jesus and His way, or sin and its course. Scripture leaves no room for doubt concerning the direction of these two paths.

*"Enter through the narrow gate. For wide is the gate and broad is the road that leads to destruction, and many enter through it. But small is the gate and narrow the road that leads to life, and only a few find it."* — Matthew 7:13-14

When one accepts God's gift of eternal life, it is the narrow path which one chooses. It requires discipline, commitment and consistency. The path of sin leads to the agony of fire, which is a destructive force of immortality. Make no mistake about this; **we will all live forever**. The eternal life is based upon the path one chooses for one's life. The wide path that leads to destruction requires no effort except to follow one's own desires.

The greatest passage used which adequately demonstrates the contrast of life direction, as well as Jesus' work as our bridge to immortality, is found in John:

*"Just as Moses lifted up the snake in the desert, so the Son of Man must be lifted up, that everyone who believes in him may have eternal life. "For God so loved the world that he gave his one and only Son, that whoever believes in him shall not perish but have eternal life."* — John 3:14-16

*"Whoever believes in the Son has eternal life, but whoever rejects the Son will not see life, for God's wrath remains on him."* — *John 3:36*

It is here that we must pause and ask the question: Do you really believe on Jesus Christ? Realizing that he is the only way of life eternal, we must truly "<u>believe</u>". <u>Believing</u> is more than a mere word. <u>Believing</u> is a practical lifestyle. Its definition is what really brings it home. By committing yourself to these three principles, you will inherit life eternal and be headed on the narrow path:

1.  To believe on Jesus Christ means that you admit you are a sinner and realize that the only reconciliation with God is through Jesus Christ.

2.  To believe on Jesus Christ means that you will turn away from your old way of doing things and make a lifelong decision to live your life for Him.

3.  To believe on Jesus Christ means that you are endeavoring to build a personal, up-to-date, day-by-day, relationship with Him.

This bridge to immortality is the key to this life as well as the life to come.

## THE WORK OF IMMORTALITY

Although it is not our own "work" by which we receive immortality, it is, nevertheless, our day-by-day effort which helps us to realize the end result of faithfulness.

*"The one who sows to please his sinful nature, from that nature will reap destruction; the one who sows to please the Spirit, from the Spirit will reap eternal life."* — *Galatians 6:8*

This battle with the flesh is a simple one where we can never win if we work within our own strength. The actual process of abolishing the work, (desire, pull and drive) of the flesh is as much a part of the spiritual world as salvation. It occurs at a point in our own decision to surrender every area of our lives to Christ. Godliness is the result.

> *"For physical training is of some value, but godliness has value for all things, holding promise for both the present life and the life to come." — I Timothy 4:8*

Godliness, as presented, is a broad concept that includes the belief in the death, burial, and resurrection of Jesus Christ, plus our own personal involvement in the propagation of this truth to the world. Different denominations may use different terms for this spiritual experience — baptism with the Holy Spirit, or sanctification, or the Lordship of Christ.

This spiritual death to the flesh is a critical experience in our work of immortality. It helps us considerably on the journey of faith. Some call this phenomenon the life of holiness. In the Christian movement through the years, we have developed certain buzzwords. "Holiness" is one in some circles. There is a scripture that looks at it.

> *"Yet you have a few people in Sardis who have not soiled their clothes. They will walk with me, dressed in white, for they are worthy." — Revelation 3:4*

The act of dying to the flesh brings a whole new lifestyle. The Apostle Paul speaks of "dying daily." Both the act of dying in a spiritual decision, as well as the daily execution, is a personal, spiritual life between a believer and God.

Often people have seen this kind of thing as impossible. The truth is, within our own strength it is impossible!

> *"He died for us so that, whether we are awake or asleep, we may live together with him." — 1 Thessalonians 5:10*

*"And give relief to you who are troubled, and to us as well. This will happen when the Lord Jesus is revealed from heaven in blazing fire with his powerful angels. He will punish those who do not know God and do not obey the gospel of our Lord Jesus. They will be punished with everlasting destruction and shut out from the presence of the Lord and from the majesty of his power."* — *2 Thessalonians 1:7-9*

Being able to realize our responsibility in this area is to simply say yes to God, accept His help and submit our lives minute by minute to Him. This is the essence of the daily work of immortality.

These two worlds of the flesh and Spirit are constantly at war with one another. There are two records as well. The system we see is the physical world. You keep track of it. Your home, car, clothes and bank account. In addition, you include all of your good deeds.

The other record is the one that is not seen. God keeps track of these books. These are all the things you do which no one sees. But God sees them and notes them.

Eternity will be a place where we will live from God's record. Everything done for Him will be rewarded. Everything done for us — or for credit — or to be noticed — has already received a reward. Only those things done for God will last forever.

I think everyone should work on this principle. So many today insist on being acknowledged, especially in the church. What we forget is that Jesus said if we have to be acknowledged, we have received our reward already.

The work for immortality is a personal, private and even secretive effort. The work for immortality will forever yield its own reward!

# THE STRUGGLE FOR IMMORTALITY

The day-to-day Christian life can be a struggle. This struggle often seems like a "struggle for immortality." Bearing in mind that we can only be successful in the struggle with God's help, there are several things we must realize in this struggle for immortality.

**First, we must realize that life is like building a building**:

> *"Fight the good fight of the faith. Take hold of the eternal life to which you were called when you made your good confession in the presence of many witnesses."* — *1 Timothy 6:12*

> *"In this way they will lay up treasure for themselves as a firm foundation for the coming age, so that they may take hold of the life that is truly life."* — *1 Timothy 6:19*

It is interesting to note that this refers to the foundation, which is the greatest reflection upon the strength of a building. A building can be extremely beautiful, but if it doesn't have a good foundation, it is doomed. We must realize that our daily struggles are provided by God to build a strong foundation within us.

**The second thing to realize is that our struggles are very small compared to eternity.**

> *"We fail to receive a hundred times as much in this present age* (homes, brothers, sisters, mothers, children and fields — and with them, persecutions) *and in the age to come, eternal life."* — Mark 10:30

Many people gripe, complain, and feel sorry for themselves when it comes to their struggles. A very important point to remember is the hardest struggle is very short in comparison to eternity.

**The third thing we must realize is we have nothing to fear. The only thing we need to be concerned with is that we please Jesus.**

> *"Do not be afraid of those who kill the body but cannot kill the soul. Rather, be afraid of the One who can destroy both soul and body in hell."* — *Matthew 10:28*

We must get our priorities right. Everything in life must give way to our desire to please Jesus. Fear is a big motivator. We fear for our job so much, we are liable to compromise anything in order to keep it. We fear rejection so much we are liable to compromise our better sense and judgment to keep a relationship intact.

In the struggle for immortality, we must please Jesus first.

**The fourth realization must be that immortality is more priceless than anything material:**

> *"What good will it be for a man if he gains the whole world, yet forfeits his soul? Or what can a man give in exchange for his soul?"* — *Matthew 16:26*

The immortal soul is a priceless commodity. Priceless in the sense that no amount of money would be worth its forfeit. The sad part about this is that many people don't consider this until it is too late.

Just as we looked at Lazarus and the rich man, people simply don't take the time to think of the agony of hell's fire. Considering that the length of eternity is beyond our mortal mind to conceive, we can't think of the soul as anything less than priceless.

**The fifth realization is that forever is a long, long time.**

> *"Surely goodness and love will follow me all the days of my life, and I will dwell in the house of the LORD forever."* — *Psalms 23:6*

Forever is inconceivable. Our mortal minds are housed within these mortal bodies which cannot think of millions and billions of years. No clock. No calendar. No time. Period.

A momentary struggle is just plain puny compared to forever. We will dwell in the house of the Lord forever if we handle the struggles of the temporary.

**The final realization in the struggle of life is God's will is the only constant.**

> *"The world and its desires pass away, but the man who does the will of God lives forever."* —1 John 2:17

> *And this is what he promised us — even eternal life.* –1 John 2:25

In the struggles of life, we must have some constants: We need to believe so hard in some things that it will carry us through any struggle. The will of God is one of those constants. The stable factor of God's will is counting upon our belief in it. Clearly the work will pass away, but God's will abides and stays constant forever. Adapting God's will through his Word helps us to acquire strength for the struggle of immortality.

## THE HOPE OF IMMORTALITY

> *"The faith and love that spring from the hope that is stored up for you in heaven and that you have already heard about in the word of truth, the gospel that has come to you. All over the world this gospel is bearing fruit and growing, just as it has been doing among you since the day you heard it and understood God's grace in all its truth."* — Colossians 1:5-6

Hope is the one thing no one can take away from you. Hope needs to be that one sustaining force which keeps us working, reaching and driving. An old saying tells us that mankind can live 40 days without food, four days without water, eight minutes without air, but only one second without hope.

> *"A faith and knowledge resting on the hope of eternal life, which God, who does not lie, promised before the beginning of time..."* — *Titus 1:2*

The greatest hope we have (which surpasses anything this world has to offer) is our hope of eternal life. **Eternal life has notoriously been the source of encouragement to Christian believers for centuries.**

This hope is simply the greatest compelling force behind our drive and desire to win the lost, as well as simple, personal obedience to the faith.

> *"Whom he poured out on us generously through Jesus Christ our Savior, so that, having been justified by his grace, we might become heirs having the hope of eternal life."* — *Titus 3:6-7*

Even our hope is not our own work or effort. The very fact we have hope is evidence of our being bought with a price. Our hope of eternal life is not just greatly linked, but supremely linked, to our justification by the grace of God through Jesus Christ. No matter how in debt, no matter how burdened, no matter what the problem; the hope of eternal life should give us a day-by-day lust for life. Even if we have troubles of our own making, hope is the touchstone.

> *"May our Lord Jesus Christ himself and God our Father, who loved us and by his grace gave us eternal encouragement and good hope,"* — *2 Thessalonians 2:16*

In early days, people were so poor and even destitute, their hope of eternal life was the only thing that kept them going. Now our times are more prosperous, but we should emulate the same faith. We should not be held captive by our bondage of materialism or materialistic desire. We must be set free to proclaim that whatever I have or possess, or shall ever have, will not free my mind and soul like my hope of eternal life.

> *"And they can no longer die; for they are like the angels. They are God's children, since they are children of the resurrection. But in the account of the bush, even Moses showed that the dead rise, for he calls the Lord 'the God of Abraham, and the God of Isaac, and the God of Jacob.' He is not the God of the dead, but of the living, for to him all are alive."*
> *—Luke 20:36-38*

The hope of eternal life can be summed up in one word: <u>life</u>. "Life and more life" is the phrase that should sum up both the present and future life of the believer. The Christian believer must exemplify the word <u>hope</u>!

## THE COMMUNION UNTO IMMORTALITY

> *"And this is the will of him who sent me, that I shall lose none of all that he has given me, but raise them up at the last day. For my Father's will is that everyone who looks to the Son and believes in him shall have eternal life, and I will raise him up at the last day."*

> *"At this the Jews began to grumble about him because he said, 'I am the bread that came down from heaven.' They said, 'Is this not Jesus, the son of Joseph, whose father and mother we know? How can he now say, 'I came down from heaven'?' 'Stop grumbling among yourselves,' Jesus answered. 'No one can come to me unless the Father who sent me draws him, and I will raise him up at the last day. It is written in the Prophets: 'They will all be taught by God.' Everyone who listens to the Father and learns from him comes to*

*me. No one has seen the Father except the one who is from God; only he has seen the Father. I tell you the truth; he who believes has everlasting life. I am the bread of life. Your forefathers ate the manna in the desert, yet they died. But here is the bread that comes down from heaven, which a man may eat and not die. I am the living bread that came down from heaven. If anyone eats of this bread, he will live forever. This bread is my flesh, which I will give for the life of the world.' Then the Jews began to argue sharply among themselves, 'How can this man give us his flesh to eat?' Jesus said to them, 'I tell you the truth, unless you eat the flesh of the Son of Man and drink his blood, you have no life in you. Whoever eats my flesh and drinks my blood has eternal life, and I will raise him up at the last day. For my flesh is real food and my blood is real drink. Whoever eats my flesh and drinks my blood remains in me, and I in him. Just as the living Father sent me and I live because of the Father, so the one who feeds on me will live because of me. This is the bread that came down from heaven. Your forefathers ate manna and died, but he who feeds on this bread will live forever.' He said this while teaching in the synagogue in Capernaum. On hearing it, many of his disciples said, 'This is a hard teaching. Who can accept it?'"* — John 6:39-60*

*"I give them eternal life, and they shall never perish; no one can snatch them out of my hand."* — John 10:28*

*"Jesus said to her, "I am the resurrection and the life. He who believes in me will live, even though he dies; and whoever lives and believes in me will never die. Do you believe this?"* — John 11:25-26*

Communion (the bread representing the body; and the juice representing the blood) may sound trivial, but it is an extremely powerful exercise. It is the one time that Jesus guaranteed He would be there when we participated together. Christ took communion so seriously that He compared it to His body that would be crucified, and His blood that would be shed. He said that when we partook, we shared in His death with Him. How powerful!

It is not coincidental that he used Passover emblems or sequences. It involved not just sacrifices, but the ultimate sacrifice. We can never over-emphasize communion. Its impact goes beyond religious tradition. It transcends any human understanding. We do it because Christ told us to do it!

I will admit to failure. It is not because I would "like" to, but because I have to. I admit to not being able to show my pastoral flock the supreme importance of the sacraments of communion. My failure was evident one Christmas Eve when I served family communion from 5:30-7:30 p.m. The regular Sunday evening worship had been canceled so that families could come and share the sacraments together. From a constituency of 150 families — 40 people came to receive. Explanations all garnered the same response — family gatherings and the exchange of gifts!

How we lose sight of what a family gathering really should be! I could easily preach a sermon about this rather than write a page, but I must force myself to bring conviction rather than stir emotion.

> "Keep yourselves in God's love as you wait for the mercy of our Lord Jesus Christ to bring you to eternal life." — Jude 1:21

Examination must not be just a once-in-a-while exercise. Instead, it must be a daily experience. Not only does daily examination of the soul keep one up to date spiritually, but also fresh and free from stagnation and lukewarmness!

## IMMORTALITY'S REWARD

*"Then he said, 'Jesus, remember me when you come into your kingdom.'"* — *Luke 23:42*

*"Jesus answered him, 'I tell you the truth, today you will be with me in paradise.'"* — *Luke 23:43*

*"He was caught up to paradise. He heard inexpressible things, things that man is not permitted to tell."* — *2 Corinthians 12:4*

The reward for faithful Christian living is immortality or eternal life. This may sound rather redundant in view of this entire chapter on immortality. Nevertheless, questions arise concerning the state of the soul between death and the judgment seat of Christ (for the believer) or the great white throne judgment (for the sinner). This entire book is to be about hell, but we would be remiss to preclude the reward of immortality — which is eternal life in God's presence.

There are basically three sources that give us our opinion regarding the soul's state at death. The first scriptural source comes to us from Jesus' first convert from the cross. The very criminal next to Jesus on the cross made a very simple request — "remember me." This man who was being crucified as a criminal very simply does the one thing we all must do to enter heaven: He looked to Jesus as his only source for eternal life. It is an interesting contrast that the criminal on one side mocks and scoffs while the one on the other side believes.

It was a simple choice. It was a personal decision. Yet, even as the man believed, he faced the humiliation of nakedness, the extreme pain of crucifixion, the mocking of the crowd, and the guilt of his own sins. Through this difficult road, he now journeyed to the Savior.

It might have been what he saw in the silent, suffering Savior. It could have been his own personal desperation. Most likely, though, it was simply his desire to rise higher. He longed for personal deliverance. He reached the right conclusion that Jesus was the only way to deliverance.

Jesus' response is our first indication of the destination of the free soul at the point of death. *"Today you shall be with me in paradise."* Jesus offered no theological argument, nor definite position paper. What he did offer is the destination of the believer at the point of death. The person who believes in Jesus as his Savior and deliverer can expect a simple transition from this world to the next. The truth in this comes from Jesus.

<u>Second</u> the Apostle Paul states in II Corinthians 5:8 – "We are confident, I say and willing rather to be absent from the body and to be present with the Lord."

It seems from this testimony of the Apostle that this absence is quite obviously death. It clearly puts the Christian believer in the framework that when one dies; one is immediately with Jesus in heaven.

Further, there seems to be no lapsing of time. It is as if the eyes were closed and reopened, closed in death and reopened unto life eternal. In all of the fussing over death, as well as the fear of death, this seems to put it all into a unique perspective.

Several years ago I was doing some seminars on handling crisis. It was during the very difficult farm crisis of the 1980's in the Midwest. I went by a men's clothing store carrying a poster with me that promoted the seminars I was giving and asked the clerk if I could put the poster up on the door or in the window. I had known this woman for some time and had known her to be a regular churchgoer, as well as a professed born-again Christian. She studied my poster for quite some time and said, "Preacher, couldn't you do a seminar on helping Christians to not fear death?"

I don't remember my response, but I do remember that it opened my eyes to something I had wrongly assumed. I assumed a Christian believer looked forward to eternal life so much that they would not fear it. As the years go by, I realize how wrong my assumption had been. Christians should see and be trained to see death as merely a transition, or merely an absence from the physical body.

Thirdly, the scriptural source of Paul's own personal experience as seen in 2 Corinthians 12:4 tells of his personal glimpse of heaven.

> *"... Was caught up to paradise. He heard inexpressible things, things that man is not permitted to tell." — 2 Corinthians 12:4*

God sent a messenger of Satan to buffet Paul so he would not become too arrogant from this great blessing of being able to see the other side.

There are many legends about the after life. I mentioned earlier a recent report someone had showed me that indicated the Soviets were drilling into the earth. At the nine-mile point, they heard some sounds. After recording the sounds and playing them back, they found the sounds to be like screams of anguish from millions of people.

Several years ago I saw a report which said scientists have discovered a "pocket" trillions of light years from earth which seems to have the depth of trillions of miles and looks to the naked eye as the lights of a city!

No matter what kind of sense we make of stories like these, it comes down to each individual's decision to either believe in immortality or not. If we don't believe, no amount of stories will change our minds. If we do believe, these kinds of stories are not necessary.

# CHAPTER 4

# "AN ICE CUBE'S CHANCE IN HELL"

## (The Warnings of Hell)

*"Meanwhile, when a crowd of many thousands had gathered, so that they were trampling on one another, Jesus began to speak first to his disciples, saying: "Be on your guard against the yeast of the Pharisees, which is hypocrisy. There is nothing concealed that will not be disclosed, or hidden that will not be made known. What you have said in the dark will be heard in the daylight, and what you have whispered in the ear in the inner rooms will be proclaimed from the roofs. "I tell you, my friends, do not be afraid of those who kill the body and after that can do no more. But I will show you whom you should fear: Fear him who, after the killing of the body, has power to throw you into hell. Yes, I tell you, fear him. Are not five sparrows sold for two pennies? Yet God forgets not one of them. Indeed, the very hairs of your head are all numbered. Don't be afraid; you are worth more than many sparrows. "I tell you, whoever acknowledges me before men, the Son of Man will also acknowledge him before the angels of God. But he who disowns me before men will be disowned before the angels of God. And everyone who speaks a word against the Son of Man will be forgiven, but anyone who blasphemes against the Holy Spirit will not be forgiven. "When you are brought before synagogues, rulers and authorities, do not worry about how you will defend yourselves or what you will say, for the Holy Spirit will teach you at that time what you should say."* — Luke 12:1-12*

Several years ago at a church I pastored, I was preparing during the Sunday school hour for my morning message.

Right next to my office the senior adult class was meeting. Often I could hear their discussions through the walls. One man named Vernon only came to Sunday school and not to the morning worship service. He was a cranky old fossil who had a negative spirit. He really didn't know what was going on at the church since he would drive up close to a rear door and leave the same way immediately after the Sunday school class was dismissed. Vernon had one special soapbox. Rarely a week would go by without his comment that would go generally like this: "Well, I ask you, when was the last sermon you heard on hell?" I remember when someone told me he had said that, I remarked, "When is he ever there in service to hear it?" Then the more often I heard him say it through the walls, the more mature my reaction became until I didn't respond at all. After all, it was God, who was supposed to tell me what to preach, wasn't it?

Well, on this one Sunday morning I could hear him clear his throat. He must have been sitting right next to my wall. The teacher was following the quarterly pretty close, and the lesson was something about the prophets. Out of the blue (after he had cleared his throat), Vernon interrupted the teacher with his usual theme, "When was the last message you heard on hell?"

I don't know if I felt especially immature, tired, frustrated, or what. I was working hard to build that church. The new sanctuary had burned down and we were rebuilding it. People were getting saved. Things were going well, but this old geezer's pickiness gnawed at me. I decided then and there to preach a series of sermons on hell.

The cutest thing happened. I preached on hell for six weeks. For a couple of weeks, Vernon was out of town. Then it took a week or so to rest up on the weekends after the trip. About the final week of my six-week series, Vernon showed up at Sunday school. About halfway through the class I could hear Vernon clear his throat, "Well," he said, "When was the last time...." The teacher interrupted him: "Vernon, look here. If you ever heard a sermon, you would know that our young preacher has been preaching on hell for weeks now." She said dogmatically, "Furthermore, would you mind keeping your opinions to yourself. I am tired of hearing about hell from him and from you!"

"Touché," I thought. Mission accomplished!

During that sermon series I came across Luke, the twelfth chapter. This passage is a real eye opener. The warnings described must be carefully heeded. There are several other Scriptures that deal with the Day of Judgment, but this one truly tries to give us some directions for areas of potential weakness. These warnings are some great principles for life. Properly applied, they not only help us to avoid the awful agony of the fire, but also create a constant challenge to live a greater spiritual existence.

Some see these sorts of things as negative. We never should see any challenge of any sort as negative. When we see in the negative, we tend to become sarcastic and cynical. God's Word must challenge us. We must see it as a spring in a desert. It must be seen and proclaimed as our road to a new and better life. Let these warnings become principles which go to work for us!

## Warning #1: Everything hidden will one day be made known. v. 2

The greatest evil of our world is deception, and Satan is the originator of it. Things done and covered over is the sum total of deception. Most of the time deception seems to work in the material world. The spiritual world is an entirely different story.

Spiritually speaking, deception does not exist because in the spiritual world, everything is done in the open. Everything is vulnerable, clear, and free. This is the world of light. Jesus keeps it that way. The physical world that we can see is really a world of darkness. This all is great irony.

When someone sees the spiritual light, they take responsibility for their sins, realizing they cannot pay the price for them on their own. They boldly accept Jesus to do so in their place. For those who resist, an awful day is in store. (We will look at great length at this "judgment day" in a later chapter.) In a courtroom setting, all of their hidden sins will be revealed. They will publicly be exposed. The sentence will be imposed — the agony of fire.

An important thing for us to address here is child abuse. Many of our children deal with episodes of life they would like to forget. Things like sexual molestation sometimes make youngsters feel guilty, dirty, or even responsible. We must be able to help these people in a constructive manner. We cannot just "not talk about it." These hidden things are suppressed deep within a child and often cause problems as an adult, but often are never dealt with.

Christian believers must become trained to help these hurting people. In developing a relationship with Christ, one is able to fill the emptiness which abuse leaves behind. I am not suggesting an easy answer or a "lead them and leave them" scenario. We must be there to help hurting people by leading them to Jesus, nurturing their relationship with Jesus, and discipling them in faith!

## Warning #2: Every secret will one-day be revealed. v. 3

Think about all the secrets you have ever had and kept — deep dark ones, personal ones, and private ones. If revealed, they would cause great pain. Everyone has secrets. In the same sense, we all have skeletons. Skeletons are secrets that involve other people. We hide these. The common way to say it is "skeleton in the closet" since the closet is where we hide many things. Maybe where things are hidden are in a drawer or behind the bathroom door. It doesn't matter where.

Our second warning is, **"Every secret will be revealed."** Think about the embarrassment and humiliation of having this happen! Many think that this time is the great Day of Judgment. Others see it as a natural course of life. Whatever you believe, it is not possible to consider never having secrets, since they seem to be such a natural part of the course of life. They are sometimes an imperative to avoid hurt in the lives of others. The only fail- safe way to avoid the revelation of the secrets in your life is to have them all blotted out.

The greatest of all doctrines is justification. The simplest way to remember the definition of justification is "just as if we never sinned." This is the blotting-out concept of Jesus' death; burial, and resurrection. When the sinner asks for forgiveness, God forgives and "remembers his sins no more." This is more than just forgetting about them, for it also requires God to think as if the sins were never committed in the first place.

Further, after one has sought forgiveness, one must live a more vulnerable, holy life. Sometimes in our Christian journey we can get sloppy in our lifestyle. By letting down our guard, we do accept things we previously would not have accepted.

Not only forgiveness and vulnerability, but also transparency must become evident in our life. Living transparently means more of an open lifestyle. It means keeping the lines open between you and God; and between you and others, by being open.  Living honestly, openly and fully will help wipe out the secrets.

## Warning #3: Don't be afraid for your life.  v. 4-5

Recently I was in the barbershop for a hair cut.  Several men were there just to chitchat and loaf.  On this particular summer afternoon, one of the men happened to be a retired local judge.  He was in his normally expressive mood.  I was listening to him rant and rave.  I knew he would eventually pick on the church in general and preachers specifically.  He didn't know who I was, nor did I expose myself.  I just listened.  Finally he said: "And what about church folks. They all want to go to heaven, but they are all afraid to die!"

Most fear comes from the ultimate feeling of fear — death. That fear is often fear of the final journey through the tunnel. From that vantage point, we also fear for lessor things like jobs, finances, and relationships.  All these fears, however, give way to that great fear of death.

Jesus' instructions give us a principle of life.  We don't have to fear death if we are a believer.  The only person we have to please is the Creator of the soul.  The practical application comes to light as we remind ourselves of this fact every day. Remember:  Don't be afraid.  God is the only one we need to please.  Don't compromise.  Don't fear.

Shirley MacLaine has helped to usher in what is referred to by many as the "New Age Movement."  The truth is the new age is the neatly packaged, highly imaged and aggressively marketed version of eastern religion and mysticism.  The very center of its belief system is a spiritual initiative that involves dying emotionally to this life and its application to not fear death.  As one achieves this state, at the point of death, one becomes a part of God.  If this state is not achieved, then the soul is reincarnated into another life form to try to "get it right." This sounds simplistic. It is an attempt to explain volumes of ancient teachings in just a few sentences, but we are amiss to overlook one of the basic truths of the Christian faith. Christianity is an eastern religion as well. At the very center of its belief system is the personal testimony of the believer which says and applies, "I no longer live, but Christ lives in me." To actually live this testimony is to so die to oneself that one fears neither life nor whatever that means, nor death and whatever the "step over" is about. Death to the believer is simply a transition — a simple step. Death to self is a simple decision.

**Warning #4: God keeps track and knows everything. v. 6-7**

"God keeps track of every time you do something bad," she said.

I was scared. I was in the second grade in children's church and Marge Osbourne was teaching us about God's record keeping system.

"What does He write on?" I inquired.

"On a big clipboard," she said. "But always remember if we ask Him to forgive us, He has the biggest old eraser you ever saw. And he erases your sins forever."

Marge Osbourne is a precious saint! She told kids about God's record keeping system as well as His forgiveness. I have never forgotten this particular session. I only wish everyone could have the same kind of spiritual event where they come face to face with God's record keeping system. Our lives, every detail, are recorded. God keeps track and knows everything. Ask yourself the question. How is your record book? Has God a need to pull out His eraser?

That God has every hair of your head numbered may not register as important to most people, but to those who have a deep, pressing need, this can create a new sensation of hope. This scripture actually creates a spirit of relief — relief to affirm what we all hoped would be so. We wish all of our prayers would be answered exactly the way we prescribe. When they aren't, we assume either that God cannot help us or that he does not care. These two conclusions do nothing but hurt our faith. We need to step above this mind set. This scripture helps us do exactly that. Our assumption as a Christian believer must be:

- That God cares deeply — more than any one else possibly could about me.

- That he knows more about every situation than I could possibly know or even have the capacity to know. For instance, I don't know how many hairs I have on my head!

- God knows every outcome, every avenue, and every action/reaction principle of everything.

Hence, we are limited. God is infinite. We must totally place our life in his hands, ask for his mercy and accept his strength and grace.

**Warning #5: Those who tell others about their faith will be protected and strengthened. Those who do not, will not!**

I have always heard it said that if we do not witness here on earth, that once we are in heaven at the judgment, Jesus would act like he does not know us. There may be quite a lot to this, but I believe in an additional application.

First, let's talk about what I call the Judgment Seat of Christ, or the judgment of/for Christians. This is the time and place where the Christian believer will be rewarded for what he/she has done. Jesus tells us in the gospels that the only difference between the sheep and the goats is what they did and didn't do. This accounting will mark the beginning of the millennial period. It will be a time of great accounting. Awards will be given, but there may be some sorrow where Christians realize they could have done so much more. Yet, even so there will be no way to go back and redo. The lessons need to be applied now. There is no need to feel any regret. Do everything you can do for Christ. It will be during this time (some call it the Marriage Supper of the Lamb), that the angels will watch in awe. Motives will be judged. It should be a tremendous learning time.

The additional application is very practical: As we witness about the saving, sanctifying power of Christ; Jesus dispatches the angels to protect us and strengthen us in our endeavors. The soul winner is the greatest enemy of Satan. People don't have to do a thing to go to hell, but they do have to be saved to get to heaven. The one who witnesses is doing the greatest work of eternity. God makes sure through Jesus that this person has all the help possible to accomplish the mission.

Those who don't witness are in fact, afraid of Jesus. He is ashamed of them as well. The sad truth is, they have no protection, support or strength.


**Warning #6: Don't blaspheme the Holy Spirit! v. 10**

This topic has had wide discussion through the years. It has even caused great fear in many. The traditional approach has been if you blaspheme the Holy Spirit, He is gone from your life forever. Further, because He is responsible for conviction of sins, you will not care about God or care that he has left you at all. Through the years of pastoring, from time to time people think they have committed this unpardonable sin. My response is always simple — if you think you might have, be assured you have not — since you still are concerned about it!

The original Greek word for blaspheme suggests the highest form of evil actions and talk. There is much more leeway than what might have been previously thought. Evil takes on many forms, and so does the blasphemy of the Holy Spirit. Evil is a progressive thing. It is all consuming. It is certainly degenerating. The blasphemy of the Holy Spirit is an ongoing, consuming, degenerative action. It is not certain words said, nor a particular way to say them. It is a spirit of the heart and that spirit is indeed very ugly.

What kinds of people have blasphemed the Holy Spirit? The first ones that come to mind are the most violent, hardened criminals who couldn't care less about Jesus. It could even be the money hungry spirit of the drug cartel. Surprisingly enough, it might even be a power-hungry church board member who is picky and critical, who may have degenerated so much from the faith that he has forgotten what is the real purpose of the Church. It could be many more, but it is not for us to point them out.

It is our responsibility to carefully safeguard our own hearts to not allow any spiritual degeneration. Check for yourself. Do you love Jesus as much as you used to love Him? Is there anything that stands between you and Jesus?

**Warning #7: Don't operate in your own power, but in the power of the Holy Spirit. v. 11-12**

Jesus left us with many profound teachings. Most importantly, He left us to carry on in His place. He clearly told his disciples that He had to go to heaven so that the Comforter could come. Jesus knew His place. He knew the Holy Spirit's place. And He gave us our place as His ambassadors to build the church. Jesus made it clear that He felt that He had given us everything we needed to carry out His orders. He has equipped us, guided and directed us. Now it is our personal responsibility to carry them out.

Our most dangerous problem is twofold:

1. To do nothing.

2. To do things in our own power and might.

If we do nothing to build the Kingdom of God of which Jesus is the cornerstone, we are defeated before we even do battle. We have given up before we started. We simply must not allow this to happen. We must look fully to Jesus for His help.

The second problem comes if we do things in our own power and might. This is what so many people do. It does not take long to wear out or burn out if you are functioning in your own strength. Many people burn out in their Christian ministry today. The reason for this is because they try to please others, don't stay close to Jesus, and they work hard in their own strength. Soon, they simply wear out!

A major reason for this burnout is simply because people want to receive too much credit. They receive the glory instead of God. God didn't create us to receive glory. So we must pass our glory back to him. We must be instruments and vessels, not possessors. Even those who have good intentions at the start end up with horrible emotional and mental problems because they put too much emphasis upon their own labor.

It is more than just taking one's self too seriously. We have placed way too much emphasis upon our own efforts!

## CONCLUSIONS ON WARNINGS

There are certainly many more things to look at concerning hell. These first few chapters help us get our feet wet. The seven warnings we have looked at should help us open our eyes to the direction we are heading. The real purpose of the warnings is to help us form a better view of life for a higher purpose.

# CHAPTER 5

## "THE HABITS OF HELL!"

*"If your hand or your foot causes you to sin cut it off and throw it away. It is better for you to enter life maimed or crippled than to have two hands or two feet and be thrown into eternal fire."* — Matthew 18:8

*"And if your eye causes you to sin, gouge it out and throw it away. It is better for you to enter life with one eye than to have two eyes and be thrown into the fire of hell."* — Matthew 18:9

"Smoking will not send you to hell," I heard it once said, "It will make you smell like you've been there!" People have all different kinds of habits, idiosyncrasies, or prejudices that are bad. But how bad are they?

Actual church denominations have been founded to exemplify one particular set of lifestyle questions. "This church or that church believes this or that" has been the talk of many. From that point, many churches split and start new churches from the basic disagreement over lifestyle issues.

In even the most fundamental, conservative churches where the people are basically in one accord, there are many serious controversies. In my ministry there have been numerous incidences of debate over habits and lifestyle. Some years ago I took into membership a man who smoked. A couple of the little old ladies made this a real issue. It took some time before their gossip made its rounds back to me. The most intriguing statement was made, "We have had to obey the rules all these years," they complained. "Why shouldn't they have to obey the rules, too?" The amusing thing about this is their apparent resentment. They "obeyed the rules" because they felt this compelling urge to go along rather than obey the rules because they were right to obey! Did these little old ladies want to smoke? No — but the sad truth is, their basis for criticism of the new member's smoking was extremely flimsy!

If we create a list of criteria of don'ts — if you will (when we measure up, we can join) — what we have is an initiation into a social club rather than into the church of the Lord Jesus Christ. Simply, if you can get to heaven, you can join a church!

Speaking of <u>heaven</u>, will habits send you to <u>hell</u>? Which ones? How will they? These are some very pertinent questions that need to be answered and which we will attempt to answer in this chapter. We are dealing with it in a rather odd point in our study of hell. The "habits of hell" come any time, at any place.

These questions are very difficult. The answers are very simple. What we have to do to answer the questions are some very stupid responses. At the very moment that I am writing the rough draft to this chapter, something is occurring in my life to illustrate this.

My wife teaches kindergarten at a private Christian school in our city. One of her little students has a parent who is a very close friend of the theater owner in town. Walt Disney's delightful movie "Jungle Book" is in town and the theater owner invited the kindergarten class in to watch it. My wife asked the parents and everyone got very excited that their children would be able to watch the movie. The only drawback is my own denomination takes a rather strong stand against going to the "movie theater." My personal stand is not as strong. I feel strongly that we must be extremely careful at what we feed our minds. I don't believe we can, nor should we try to dictate behavior to people. Nevertheless, my wife did not wish to run the risk of the judgmental tendencies of many of our church people finding out that she went to see the "Jungle Book." If she went, and they found out, it could cause great trouble for my ministry. So right now, she is sitting at her desk while her students are at the movie with their room mothers as chaperons.

How many times have you avoided doing something just to avoid the fussing of other Christians? Sometimes we as Christians have hurt the cause of Christ more than we have helped!

What type of activities could send us to hell? This question really is the bottom line. The breath of Scripture shows us that we are all born into sin, and that without Christ, we are condemned. Do our habits condemn us? The simple answer would be an individual answer; but yes, our habits could condemn us to hell. We could be condemned if we neglect to listen to God's voice, become hardened, and cut ourselves off from God. It can happen. It does happen!

This scenario of degeneration will be looked at in a much greater extent in a later chapter. When it comes to habits, the scenario begins when we start <u>not listening to God as much</u>. This creates a need that one usually fills with some kind of habitual behavior. The human spirit is such that when there is emptiness, it will get filled up with something.

The second part of this habit-forming scenario is a <u>spiritual hardening.</u> When one hardens spiritually, it takes the form of mental and intellectual justification. Our minds can literally justify any behavior. During this hardening stage, habits develop and can form a foothold in a life.

The third part of degeneration is the cutting off of the relationship with Jesus Christ. During this point, even those very hardened spiritually know that there are big problems. But they are to the point that they don't care. This scenario can be applied to any behavior that works its way between us and our relationship with God.

Jesus gives some very strong directions about habits: "cut it off!" This was an especially stirring challenge to people with offensive behavior. I shouldn't use the word "was", but "is". I want to explain what Jesus is saying by expanding upon what Jesus said.

We must remember that Jesus constantly spoke to people who were great hypocrites. These were people who said one thing, but did something else. They would publicly castigate a person caught in sin, but secretly do something far worse. Jesus' approach had to be strong, hard line — even brash and abrupt. He said, "If your hand offends you, cut it off!" Behind His back, they would call Jesus a vulgar and violent communicator. Jesus' intention was one of true love. He cared more that they changed their ways and avoided eternal damnation, than He did that they "liked" him.

Jesus' challenge leads us to consider anything in our behavior that would offend, transgress His will, or create a break in our relationship with Him. We must carefully safeguard our behavior. These safeguards which follow are meant to do exactly that.

The first safeguard to avoid the habits of hell has to do with your personal relationship with Jesus. One's relationship with God through Jesus Christ **must be viewed and established as a top priority** in one's life. If Jesus is not first place in your life, then your habitual behavior may become first place.

A personal relationship with Jesus is not a mystical thing as many may make it sound. It is no sillier than prayer. The relationship is based upon the premise that He lives within me and represents me to the Creator. He is my advocate to the Father. We pray to God in Jesus' name.

How is your relationship with Jesus? Not what is the strength or the power, but <u>how</u> is the place. What place does it have in your life?

**The first safeguard is to ask yourself: Is there anything in my life which stands between me and my relationship with the Lord?** Anything?

**The second safeguard to avoiding the habits that could send you to hell is to determine to glorify God in all things.** This concept is not just preventative medicine, but leads to an aggressive spiritual life of growth.

The most mature thing a Christian believer can ask himself on a periodic basis is, Will this bring glory to God? If it involves a decision, How will this situation/decision bring glory to God? If it involves habitual behavior, does this habit bring glory to God?

Bringing glory to God is what being a follower of Jesus is all about. Accepting him as Savior is not something we do to purchase a ticket to heaven and thereby avoid hell. Entering into a relationship with Jesus means to be completely His, not <u>partially</u> His. When we "no longer live, but Christ lives in us" as the Scripture says, we bring glory to God.

When we determine to bring glory to God in all we do, in all we say, in all we think, and in how we live — we perform this second safeguard perfectly. Bringing glory to God must be our goal.

**The third safeguard to avoiding the habits that could send you to hell is to carefully monitor your thought life.** Our thoughts are our very personal, private world. No one can monitor your thoughts but you. God is the only other being who knows what you are thinking. Satan is not privy to your thoughts, for he is a created being. Always remember that Satan can implant your mind with thoughts in the unseen, unconscious/conscious world, but he never knows he has "gotten through" unless we act on those thoughts.

Further, when temptations come, Satan never knows if he "has you" until you act. At that point, he never really knows it will become a habit unless you do it regularly. The more we act on it, the more we have given in to the great pull of Satan. For Satan will work that much harder for you to develop bad or unbecoming habits if he sees a weakness.

Monitoring your thoughts can nip many potential habits in the bud. We have the power to not only monitor ourselves, but to change our own behavior as well. God has given us all a mind that programs what we do. It is up to us to monitor our programs.

**The fourth safeguard to help us avoid the habits that could send us to hell, is to inventory our life often.** We must take an honest inventory, however. Taking inventory of one's lifestyle is deeply personal. The more honest one is, the more beneficial inventory taking becomes.

The text Jesus uses to talk about habitual behavior involves two parts of the body — the hand and the eyes. Of course, he could have used many other potential sources of problems, but he picked the symbol of power — the hand; as well as the symbol of lust — the eye.

Each of us must give careful attention to avoid the struggles of power, pride, and lust. These areas of struggle are typical backwashes of the day-to-day human dynamic. A typical personal inventory will involve three questions. These may be asked once a month or once an hour, depending upon the person and the need.

> ➢ Am I starting to be preoccupied with anything?
> ➢ Is something starting to consume my thinking or my time?

> Am I developing into a better/stronger person or a weaker/fragile person?

Your own inventory may depend upon you personally. An inventory is strictly a safeguard. It is meant to keep us in touch with ourselves as well as in "tow" as far as our lifestyle is concerned.

**The fifth safeguard to help us avoid the habits of hell is to swiftly remove potential danger.** Common sense could take over at this point. For instance, if you know something is a weakness, then avoid it! If you know something or someone could get you into trouble, go out of your way to stay away. Frankly, use the brain God gave you to avoid dangers to your lifestyle which could influence the eternal destiny of your soul.

Many people have been easily dissuaded here. At first they ask, "What is the harm?" And at first it appears like there is no harm. But in reality the problems are covered over and the harm is a growing, surging evil made manifest in habitual behavior.

The condition for overcoming a habit is basically a personal decision. It is not something we can do for others, nor should we ever try. We must train ourselves to never be judgmental about someone's habits. The overcoming of a habit is personal and must, repeat, **must** be treated that way.

Jesus tells us to "cut the thing off!" The reason is that it is better to be half a person and to have dealt with the habit, than to put on an appearance and have the habit send you to hell. How you look or what others think about you is in no way as important as taking care of a potentially dangerous situation.

This safeguard could mean many things. It may mean to cut off a relationship. It could mean to break off a friendship. It might mean changing a job or relocating in another city.

Whatever the price, if it is to avoid a habit, it is worth it. It must be done.

Finally, dealing with a potentially dangerous habit or a habit you have been caught up in is as simple <u>as turning it over to God.</u> Visualize yourself turning this situation over to God, even hand it to him. Let your problem be His problem from here on out. Ask Him to give you the strength. Then take it a day at a time. Concentrate on today. Today is all you have to worry about!

> ➢ Visualize turning it over to God.

> ➢ Ask for strength to overcome.

> ➢ Concentrate only on today.

The habits of hell can be avoided if they haven't started. They can be dealt with if you are starting. The habits can be overcome, if they seem to have a foothold in your life.

By applying these safeguards, you can do what Jesus said to do — "Cut it off and throw it away!"

# CHAPTER 6

# "GO TO HELL"

*"Gabriel, today is the day! Blow your horn!"*

I don't know exactly how God will say it, but when He does, every believer in Christ throughout the world will be called to the throne.

This period is a very special time between the redeemed and God that is called the "Judgment Seat of Christ." Every ounce of spirituality will be called away from the earth. This will be a season where the believers will be "debriefed." Their faith will be checked. They will give an account of their Christian lives. God will see His church in a penetrating, honest light.

Next, He will make His organizational plans for the millennial kingdom, and then for all of eternity. To those who used faithfully and well what they were given, more will be given. To those who were slothful and lazy with what they had, it will be taken away. Image and interest, politics and persuasion will stand naked before God at the judgment seat. The Church will stand naked. Many of those who were great leaders will be judged by motive. Some will not be given much responsibility in eternity because they did not use what they did have to the glory of God. The believers whom God will be able to use are the faithful servants. Those are the people who are always there without regard to credit or acknowledgement. Those are the ones who were consistently reaching out to hurting people.

The Church is what is referred to as the bride of Christ. The bridegroom is Christ. The bride will be presented to the groom as perfect at the marriage supper, at the conclusion of the Judgment Seat of Christ. This judgment seat is where God will put the "finishing touches" on His bride. He will make right the wrongs, and purge the bride of impropriety. The bride will be in perfect shape after the judgment seat of Christ.

The Church, in its present shape, is sorry-looking. Politics and power have wreaked havoc. There are so many examples of wolves in sheep's clothing. Christianity has become a multi-billion dollar industry. With all the money that changes hands, the Church seems to be more like a prostitute than a bride. Rest assured all this will be purged by the time of the presentation of the bride to the bridegroom. It behooves every believer to keep a constant assessment of his or her motives. Motives play the biggest part of why we do what we do. This Judgment Seat of Christ, and subsequent Marriage Supper of the Lamb, could be a glorious day to many. We can greatly look forward to this day as we follow Jesus' admonishment to follow Him — "Deny yourself, take up your cross, and follow me!"

## Meanwhile, Down on Earth…

Meanwhile, down on earth, every ounce of spiritual influence is gone. The salt of the earth and the light of the world are no more. This is the seven-year period called the "Great Tribulation." Politics, manipulation and deceit will rule. A world leader will rise out of Europe. The whole world will follow him. This world leader will have his own agenda.

The first three and a half years will seem great, but the second three and a half years; hell will literally break loose. There will be a war to end all wars. In the Valley of Meggido, the armies of the world will meet. This war will be the aggregate of all human hate and violence. Every evil will be made manifest. The Antichrist leader of the world will lead everyone to hell.

As the Valley of Meggido fills with blood as every possible world catastrophe is occurring, and while the demons of hell have had their seven year heyday, God will turn to Gabriel one more, final time and say, "Gabriel! Blow your horn!"

> Then I saw a great white throne and him who was seated on it. Earth and sky fled from his presence, and there was no place for them. And I saw the dead, great and small, standing before the throne, and books were opened. Another book was opened, which is the book of life. The dead were judged according to what they had done as recorded in the books. The sea gave up the dead that were in it, and death and Hades gave up the dead that were in them, and each person was judged according to what he had done. Then death and Hades were thrown into the lake of fire. The lake of fire is the second death. If anyone's name was not found written in the book of life, he was thrown into the lake of fire.  — Revelation 20:11-15

Referred to as the "Great White Throne Judgment," this event pulls many things together. Genesis 3:8-13 illustrates God's two questions to Adam, which is the whole purpose of the Great White Throne. Keep in mind the Christians are already judged. They are standing behind God on the other side of God and eternity.

Two questions God asks everyone:

1. Where are you?

2. What is it you have done?

> "Then the man and his wife heard the sound of the LORD God as he was walking in the garden in the cool of the day, and they hid from the LORD God among the trees of the garden. But the LORD God called to the man, 'Where are you?' He answered, 'I heard you in the garden, and I was afraid because I was naked;

*so I hid.' And he said, 'Who told you that you were naked? Have you eaten from the tree that I commanded you not to eat from?' The man said, 'The woman you put here with me — she gave me some fruit from the tree, and I ate it.' Then the LORD God said to the woman, 'What is this you have done?' The woman said, 'The serpent deceived me, and I ate.'"*
— *Genesis 3:8-13*

*"After he drove the man out, he placed on the East Side of the Garden of Eden cherubim and a flaming sword flashing back and forth to guard the way to the tree of life."* — *Genesis 3:24*

## Where are you?

God asked Adam, "Where are you?" Adam was hiding — embarrassed because he had disobeyed God. God asks all of humanity the same question. Jesus said, "If I am lifted up, I will <u>draw</u> all men unto me."

"Where are you?" is a drawing question. When God asks it of people, they have a choice: to either acknowledge where they are spiritually or to continue to hide from God.

When God turns to Gabriel the final time to blow his horn, He is asking the question to all created souls, "Where are you?" Instantly, in a fraction of a second, in the twinkling of an eye, they will be in God's presence.

I believe that God asks this question of us every day of our lives. Every day we breathe, the Holy Spirit asks us, "Where are you?" Where am I spiritually? Sometimes I am naked. Sometimes I hide. Sometimes I sleep right through the day.

God is asking the question right now — "Where are you?" Where are you spiritually? Many will go through their lives hiding. There is coming a day when no one can hide and all must answer. It will be a day of trial. It will be the great

Day of Judgment. On that day, God will call all of sinful humanity before himself. He will ask, "Where are you?" There will be no hiding. There will be no secrets. Everything will be laid bare. Everyone will give an account of his or her lives. Everyone great and small, rich and poor, sick and healthy, jock and brain — everyone will give an account!

Throughout Scripture there are different scenarios of the Great White Throne Judgment scene. One Jesus describes is the harvest from a fruit tree. Another illustration Jesus used was the separation of the sheep and the goats. What is so interesting about Jesus' teaching is that he clearly shows the only difference between the sheep and the goats is between what they did and did not do. We must never forget to ask, search, seek, and most importantly, <u>know</u> where we are spiritually!

**What is this you have done?**

Now comes the period of questioning. God wants to find out what is wrong. Genesis 3:10 says Adam was afraid because he was naked. Before God, we stand naked. Nothing is hidden. We may be able to fool everyone else, but God sees. He sees our every move. He knows our every thought. As God opens the Books on that Day of Judgment, people will be naked. God is a great record keeper. All things are recorded. It will be a trial. All this will be laid bare. God will show us all the times He asked for us, but we hid from Him. One by one, we will stand before the great white throne and the One who sits on it with feet of brass, hair of shining glory, Jesus Christ. We will give account.

Genesis 3:12 gives Adam's response to God. Blame. He blamed the disobedience on his wife. He further blamed it on God for giving him the woman.

Many, many people are blaming things on God. Many blame things on others. Tons of people will stand before God blaming things on others, not fully realizing the blame really rests on them.

Even as God questioned the woman, she placed blame on the serpent and then had to say, "I did eat." One thing I am absolutely sure of: At the throne of God, everyone will have to confess: "I did eat." *("All have sinned and come short of the glory of God."* — *Romans 3:23)*

Many good people who did many good things will stand before God. But being good is not enough. God will open up the Book of Life to look for your name. Anyone whose name is not written in the Book of Life will be cast into the lake of fire.

Is your name written in the Book of Life?

## Are you going to Hell?

<u>It is a question!</u> Many believe it is luck or chance that someone makes it to heaven. If that were the case, why would God bother having a judgment? Why would God bother asking the first two questions? Your answer to the first two questions will determine how you answer the last.

Genesis 3:24 says, *"So he (God), drove out the man."* Man rebelled and suffered the consequences. Man will never again return to that state.

At the great white throne, God will again ask the question, "Where are you going?" The answer will come from the Book of Life. This book will contain names and dates. The dates will be when a person met God in a personal way and found forgiveness of sins. It will record that time he "trusted" Christ. "Trust" is indeed the key to <u>eternal life.</u>

# Hell and Death will be cast into the Lake of Fire

This concept is the greatest of the Bible. God will, once and for all, eliminate evil. How will He? God will eliminate this whole dimension of the physical, as we know it. He created it, and He will eliminate it.

This laboratory called Earth and the experiment called Man will cease. God created the dimension of "light" in Genesis 1:3. God brought something finite into his creation of infinity.

The speed of light is 186,000 miles per second or 6 trillion miles per year. If you would get into a space ship and project from the earth at the speed of light; for every day that elapsed in your spacecraft as you propelled away from the earth at the speed of light, 1,000 years would elapse on earth. In ten years, you would be four million earth years old. Yet, that is just a moment in infinity: for "a day is a thousand years" to the Lord, and further "a thousand years is a day." The point is, in the spiritual realm, there is no time or space. Hell was a place prepared for the devil and his angels (Matthew 25:41), and death was prepared for man (Genesis 3:24). Both will be thrown together into the lake of fire and sulfur. Fire means a purging torture, and sulfur illustrates eternity. Sinful man's destiny is the lake of fire.

"I don't believe a loving God would send people to hell!", a lady proclaimed in the middle of philosophy class. What was so interesting was this class was full of atheists. Her statement, however, stuck with me. There is something we must understand. The lady is right! A loving God will not send anyone to hell. The whole purpose of the lake of fire is to purge the world of sin. Because people have chosen the way of sin, they are in a spiritual sense, attached to sin. It is sin God is purging. The people who are cast into the lake of fire have chosen to attach themselves to sin. A loving God clearly loves the sinner. But he greatly hates the sin. It is sin that causes the trouble. The lake of fire is created for death, hell and sin. It is the dimension that will continually purge the world of sin forever. Never again will sin be a problem.

The believer will become the bride of Christ forever and will continue on to greater assignments and capacities. The immortal soul in eternity will be in a state of absolute fulfillment. The error we have made through the years is we picture heaven as some kind of celestial retirement center. Many believe that in heaven we will do whatever we want. This attitude negates every principle of Scripture. God has paid a very high price to redeem us and help us on our spiritual journey to progress and mature. I don't believe it is His intention to allow us an eternity to sit around.

Those who are cast into the lake of fire will be purged forever. It is hard for us to conceptualize how long forever is. This Lake of Fire will continue throughout eternity.

Years ago at a youth rally, the speaker began his sermon by having us imagine our finger burning, then our hand, arm, torso, and finally our whole body on fire. Then he directed us to think of having no relief forever and forever; continual burning, agony and torment with no relief from the suffering. He preached on and on and had a big response for his altar call.

I have never been able to get over his illustration. The hardest part about the lake of fire is to know there is nothing that can be done to change the conditions. It burns on forever and forever. For all of eternity, those people will go back over and over how things could have been different. With all the regret, no change will come. Destiny will have been decided.

Now is the time to challenge people. Where are you? What have you done? People must consider these questions. We must be the ambassadors of Christ to bring these challenging questions to the people.

# CHAPTER 7

## "HELL BENT"

"You boys are hell bent!" Old Mr. Dunlavey yelled after us as we left his yard for the final time. We were 10, 11, and 12 years old. I wanted to start making some real money, so I went door to door asking for lawns to mow. Mr. Dunlavey at 1414 Agency was the only job I could land. He offered the three of us $1 to mow and bag his grass. Start to finish, it took the three of us three hours. Even in 1970, this was terrible money, but we had work, so we worked hard.

Mr. Dunlavey was a taskmaster. He would come out for continual inspection, puffing on his very large and very smelly Cuban cigars. If something was not quite right, he would launch out on a tirade about our hormones, our workmanship and finally how hell bent we were.

I knew he was an old man and we wanted the dollar, but I didn't understand "hell bent." I knew enough about hell to know I never wanted to go there. Further, I certainly didn't want to be "bent" toward going there either.

I asked my father about Mr. Dunlavey's word. It aggravated my father. Dad felt like we were good boys. (Of course, children are just an extension of their parent's pride.) My father felt like we should quit the job immediately. However, we calmed him down.

The final time we saw Mr. Dunlavey was on a very hot summer day in July. He called us up to mow his grass. While we were working, he came out. My brother had accidentally done something that irritated Mr. Dunlavey. It was 101 degrees, and extremely humid. The closer I got to Mr. Dunlavey; I could hear what the problem was. My brother was sitting under a big, shaded oak tree. Mr. Dunlavey thought sitting there would hurt the roots. He got extremely carried away, like he hadn't taken his medication, or had taken too much of it. I had enough, so I told my other brother to bring the mower over. It was then Mr. Dunlavey told us he wasn't going to pay us the three times we mowed because my brother sat under his oak tree.

Being the spokesman, I told him to find some other hell-bent slaves. Then my brother told him that hell was too nice of a place for him to spend eternity. Then we never saw Mr. Dunlavey ever again!

This word, "hell bent" has always intrigued me. I used to picture a drug-crazed hood in a back alley. Then I realized that hell already has a grip on the drug addict. How about someone slipping from the faith? This person is degenerating, which is another kind of hell bound manifestation, but it is not really hell-bent.

It isn't easy to interpret hell bent, but we must try! First we must put out of our minds certain personality types or behaviors which would seem to be hell-bent, so that we may fairly explore the concept. Being hell bent is not a boy with a slingshot. It is not Dennis the Menace. It is not a freckle-faced, wide-toothed grin. "Hell bent" is a spirit. It is the motivation behind an action. It often "comes" and "goes." Being hell bent is unpredictable. One might do great spiritual things. Then all of a sudden, circumstances change and one does things, or thinks things, or becomes things that were previously unimaginable.

Boiling it all down, being hell bent is something we should constantly be on guard about. It is an unpredictable spirit that comes upon us from time to time. It lends itself to distracting us from the still small voice and the narrow road. If we had to condense it, there are three telltale signs of the hell-bent spirit: pride, power and peer pressure. These things may not send you to the lake of fire, but they are able to cause your life to degenerate in that direction.

Pride, power and peer pressure must be viewed as powerful enemies. War must be declared against them.

## PRIDE

Several years ago I was looking for a car to buy. I came across a company executive car at the Lincoln dealership. The car was the new Mark VII. For several days, I test drove it. I loved the car, the ride, the look, and the image. I decided against the car for fear that my parishioners would resent it. When I took the car back to the dealer, he wanted to know why I decided against it. I explained that as a pastor I wanted to be careful of the feelings of my people. He then told me about the last person who test-drove it. The dealer was quite disgusted with this wealthy man who brought the car back without buying it. This customer told the dealer that he had decided to buy the car, but that morning he was reading from his devotional book of meditations. On that particular morning, the devotional meditation was about pride. It evidently hit this customer right between the eyes. He told the car dealer the only reason he wanted the Lincoln over a nice Chevrolet, was pride. He didn't buy it.

The car dealer expressed disbelief. He simply could not understand what could be wrong with pride. I can still remember him echoing some motivational speaker he heard talk about pride. "What is wrong with pride in yourself?" he asked me.

*"Therefore this is what the Sovereign LORD says: Because it towered on high, lifting its top above the thick foliage, and because it was proud of its height, I handed it over to the ruler of the nations, for him to deal with according to its wickedness. I cast it aside,"*
— *Ezekiel 31:10-11*

Society has made pride to be in vogue. We have even harnessed it, marketed it, and promoted it to be the answer to success. We produce the inward drive by venting the pride of life into our work efforts. Pride in yourself is the essence of what the motivation movement is all about. It has completely permeated the thinking of America. To suggest that pride is bad is un-American.

**The first thing we must do is to differentiate between two kinds of pride.** The first kind of pride is the pride of life. This suggests pride in your accomplishments, in things, and in yourself. This kind of pride is generally carnal. It is generally carnal rather than specifically carnal, depending upon where the pride is placed.

The second kind of pride is the mellow version. It is the pride of potential. This is the healthy form of pride. It is simply a sense of self-esteem. It is not pride of something; it is pride as something. This gives you enough pride to function on a day by day basis.

**The second thing we must do about pride is to realize its place.** Let me say something that might sound radical. If you have Jesus, you don't need pride. If you truly have Jesus, you won't have pride. The interesting thing about life in the Savior is how all consuming He is in our lives. With him in our lives, pride is totally unnecessary. If I belong to Him, I will glorify him. Pride is simple self-glory. The child of God does not glory in the flesh.

When a Christian believer starts to display pride, he/she is truly becoming "hell bent." Solomon wrote that pride comes before a fall. The entire concept of the Christian life is to be emptied of self. When one is emptied of self, pride is never a problem.

**The third thing we must do about pride is to watch out for its dangers.** There are several danger signals for the approaching concern of pride:

**Sensitivity**. People who are easily hurt are victims of pride. A person who is emptied of self has two sensitivities. Developing a sense of God's ownership, as well as a sense of humor, will go a long way to help to develop the right type of sensitivity.

➤ **Defensiveness**. Being defensive is a sure sign of pride. Never being able to admit a mistake, never being able to apologize, never accepting responsibilities, are serious character problems brought about through defensiveness. People who are defensive rarely are able to admit they have any problem at all. These people need love and understanding. A defensive person needs to feel accepted and appreciated.

➤ **Clannishness**. This is really an extension of defensiveness more acutely defined. "Clannish" means to be defensive about your family. Family members seem to merely be an extension of another's pride. I remember not long ago hearing of a preacher who went to the parking lot of the local high school to pick his sons up, only to find the both of them in a full fledged brawl with two other brothers. The preacher/father jumped out of the car only to start exchanging punches with the boys fighting with his sons. He didn't try to pull them apart or find out what the problem was, he just assumed his own sons were right. Later, he found out his son had stolen the lunch of one of the other boys.

We often get so clannish that it doesn't matter who is right or wrong just as long as they are family. Clannishness is wrong because it is a form of pride.

➤ **Conceit**. Do you know people who are constantly telling you of their good works? These people have a problem with pride. They want the world to notice them and know of their accomplishments. People who brag about themselves, or boast of their accomplishments are the most obvious ones filled with pride.

- ➤ **Jealousy**. Jealousy is another form of pride. We must be able to be happy for people who come upon good fortune. Rarely is this the case.

- ➤ **Vanity**. Vanity is having to look just right, or putting on the right appearance. Being vain is the most consuming form of pride. It can eat a person up with the passion of looking just right. Coupled with this is the right image — making sure you project just the right thing.

There could be many more things to watch out for, but each of us must do our own personal work to overcome pride.

## POWER

Secondly, but not less important or less dangerous, is the spirit of power. The spirit of power will most certainly create a bent toward hell, no matter where the power is made manifest.

Types of power vary in the widest sense of the imagination. The sense of power can be derived from being a world leader or even from flipping on a light switch. It is not what the action is; it is the attitude in the action that determines the seriousness of the spirit of power.

### The feeling of power tends to cause corruption.

Mankind was created to live in a garden. The purpose of our creation was, and still is, to bring glory to God. Power brings no glory to God, for only He should be our source of power. Humankind always becomes corrupted whenever they sense they have power.

The serpent tempted Eve with power. The tempter told her if she ate of the tree she would have God's power. That one thing sounded good to her — power. It clearly shows that she not only ate to achieve God's power, but her search for power corrupted her flesh.

Power corrupts our bodies by making us do things and attempt things beyond our mortal limits. Power corrupts our minds by making us think things about ourselves, our potential, and our own strength, which is not true. Power corrupts our souls by making us believe that we don't need God.

### The feeling of power tends to make us feel independent.

Have you ever heard the phrase "self-made man?" I worked for a man who was called a self-made millionaire. I mowed his lawn for $2. He lived in a million-dollar mansion on 100 acres. He raised Arabian racehorses. He drove a Rolls Royce convertible. I met him one time. He was driving in one day after work. I was walking my mower across the lawn. He beeped his horn at me twice and I walked over.

"Sonny," he said. "Be sure your mowers are shut off from 5:30-6:00 since I watch the news!" And off he drove! Mr. Fitzmorris didn't need anyone. He was self-made and independent.

This sort of thinking heads us straight for hell. When we think of ourselves as independent, we most certainly are "hell bent." No one is ever totally independent. We are always dependent upon God. We may be able to fool others, or even ourselves, but we cannot fool God.

### The feeling of power tends to consume us.

The more power we get, the more we want. The more we get, the more it consumes. The spirit of power is a consumer. We always need more. What we have is never enough.

A couple of elections ago, I noticed many of the nation's governors were running for president. Politics has become a stepping stone game. This is unfortunate. Why can't a good governor keep being a good governor, rather than spend two millions dollars to see if he has a shot at being the president? Why can't a good mayor keep being a good mayor? Why do we have to allow the spirit of power to consume us? Alexander the Great was the perfect example of a man with no new worlds left to conquer.

Jesus gave us explicit direction concerning power. He told us to be servants. A servant has no incarnate power. Instead, the servant of God is able to develop something far greater than power — spiritually. The ironic twist is when one becomes a servant, he is one with Christ. Being united with Christ creates the ultimate of all power — the power of God.

People will always want to dominate others. They will continue to covet power and attempt continually to "lord" over others. They will also be "hell bent" as they do. The person who wants to do well must sling off the spirit of power like a hated enemy. Power is our enemy. The spirit of power is the ultimate adversary of the Christian believer. Servanthood, submission and sacrifice are our "powerful" comrades.

## PEER PRESSURE

Some things never change! Having gone to several high school football games, I am always reminded that the hardest pressure on one's life is from one's peers. Peer pressure can be outward and overt or unspoken and covert.

Years ago I remember the antics we went through as adolescents. In my junior high school, the kids walked the halls in one direction for the boys and the opposite direction for the girls. Who you hung out with was everything. The girl who you were "going with" or the boy you were "going with" determined how cool (or not) you were.

As time passed, so did the complexity of peer pressure. During the high school years, the cool kids sat around before school in the cafeteria. Somehow, in some way, some unseen force takes over to develop a "pecking order" or a progressive order of coolness." I don't really know how it developed, but everyone knew who was number one, number two, three, and so on. The coolest eight sat at a table in the center of the cafeteria. The number one coolest dude sat in the very center on the side that faced the doors. The number two guy sat next to him, leaning in. The number three guy sat on the other side leaning in. Everyone leaned in except the center guy who was number one. The tables around this main table were also a part of the game. These were guys trying to be "cool", but weren't quite there. They would all lean, act cool, and try to be a part of the main table. What was also interesting was that the group of guys was always seasonal. During football season, the football players were setting around the tables. During basketball season, it was the basketball players.

One thing I learned by all this — popularity is fleeting. Being accepted by one's peers, as important as it may seem at the time, lasts only for a short period. Yet so many people do so many things which change their lives forever because of the silly, "hell-bent" attitude of peer pressure.

It is not only children or young people who get caught up in peer pressure. It affects adults as well. Peer pressure is very powerful because it directly meets needs in the lives of people. These needs seem to be met by peer approval. It is extremely difficult to overcome peer pressure if one does not get these needs met somewhere else.

**The need to feel needed.**

The need to feel needed is the most basic part of the human personality. When a person feels needed, it provides him with a place to belong. Everyone has an innate need to belong. The need to feel needed transcends many of the other needs in life. Some people will do things they never thought they would do if they could just feel needed. Others will break laws. Criminal gangs that do hideous things develop in many cities. Each gang member is loyal to death because each feels needed. Many people morally decay because of the need to feel needed. To change people's behavior in a constructive manner, we must be able to meet this need!

**The need for attention.**

Everyone has a need to be attended to. We all need attention. Some people need more attention than others, based upon many criteria. Peer pressure meets this need. I can remember all the different group names given to different groups in high school: the jocks, the brains, the gear head, the proud crowd, and so on. People belong to a group to have some attention given them by others. Many do criminal things just for attention.

We must do what we can to direct people toward the Lord Jesus. Helping people understand that a personal relationship with the Lord Jesus will help them to meet this need, will go a long way in breaking the power of peer pressure.

I notice this need among adults at the school my boys attend. The need for attention is great among parents in this upper middle class school district. Volvo's, BMW's, Corvettes, designer clothes, etc. mark people who are very concerned about their image and what others think. Their need to be noticed is just fulfilling their need for attention.

**The need to be loved.**

Teenage pregnancy is at an all-time high because girls just want to be loved. The boys have their lines down so pat they have learned how to manipulate and use this need to be loved.

The need to be loved is found within the bond of a peer group. It is amazing, even magical how love seems to be expressed and exemplified in a peer group.

Peer pressure is more than just pressure. It meets needs and creates in us the tendency to become hell bent. Our society has become one to be influenced, rather than to influence. It is indeed the wheel that squeaks the most which gets the most grease; so the one who speaks the loudest seems to get the most followers.

We have also become "blenders". We blend into the crowd. Much like the day in which Christ was crucified, people seem to blend into the crowd. Where were the ones Christ touched during His crucifixion? They blended into the crowd. Where were the ones Christ healed? They blended into the crowd. Where were His closest followers? They blended.

If we are really going to be the salt of the earth and the light of the world like He told us to be, we need to be influencers, not be influenced. We need to stop following someone else's path, and blaze our own path and leave a trail.

There are no alternatives. We are accountable to God for our associations. Don't let yourself be hell bent by succumbing to peer pressure.

An illustration of pride, power and peer pressure is found in the Gospel of Mark:

> *"Then James and John, the sons of Zebedee, came to him. 'Teacher,' they said, 'we want you to do for us whatever we ask.' 'What do you want me to do for you?' he asked. They replied, 'Let one of us sit at your right and the other at your left in your glory.' 'You don't know what you are asking,' Jesus said. 'Can you drink the cup I drink or be baptized with the baptism I am baptized with?' 'We can,' they answered. Jesus said to them, 'You will drink the cup I drink and be baptized with the baptism I am baptized with, but to sit at my right or left is not for me to grant. These places belong to those for whom they have been prepared.' When the ten heard about this, they became indignant with James and John. Jesus called them together and said, 'You know that those who are regarded as rulers of the Gentiles lord it over them, and their high officials exercise authority over them. Not so with you. Instead, whoever wants to become great among you must be your servant, and whoever wants to be first must be slave of all. For even the Son of Man did not come to be served, but to serve, and to give his life as a ransom for many.'"* — Mark 10:35-45

The disciples were constantly wondering when Jesus was going to "make His move" politically. It was all they knew. Jesus was gaining an immense following and enjoying great popularity from the people. These men wanted their efforts and loyalties to be rewarded. As was their culture, they thought only in external terms. They would often wonder and talk among themselves as to what they were getting out of all of this. The spirit of pride was the most common form of expression. How others perceived one represented their public persona. When the disciples saw Jesus' following grow, so did the spirit of pride, which was made manifest in their sense of expectation.

It was with this sense of expectation, or the spirit of pride, with which the two brothers, James and John, approached Jesus. It is interesting to note that they, along with Peter, were already part of Jesus' inner circle. These were the men Jesus called upon several times to unite with Him to garner extra special strength. But they wanted something for themselves. It was the spirit of pride within themselves that caused them to initiate a request for power. When these two brothers asked Jesus for special position, they were in effect requesting power for themselves as well. These two brothers were not satisfied with how things were. The wanted to be assured of future power. Working together, they approached Jesus with a need for a special favor. They were actually being wily when they asked, "Would you grant us a request?" even before they told Him what the request concerned.

Jesus knew right away these two young brothers did not understand what He was all about. They were looking for an outward, visible kingdom. Christ stood for an internal, spiritual kingdom. This conflict Jesus constantly faced during His earthly ministry. The spirit of pride and the spirit of power have no part in the kingdom of God. This request stands in stark contrast to Jesus' total mission.

The response Jesus gave them is remarkable. "You do not know what you ask." These two young brothers were still very immature. But they would not be immature forever. They would eventually drink the cup of suffering. They would propagate the gospel into the entire known world. They would also be baptized with His baptism. Spiritually speaking, they would one day understand.

*"...It is for those whom it is prepared..."* Jesus responded. We can only assume the meaning of Jesus' insight into this

eternal destination of position. Many call this statement Jesus' indication of predestination. I really believe it is more "hands on" than that concept. The positions in eternity are somehow given to those who do the most for Jesus. The preparation process is constantly taking place every hour of every day. Our response to Jesus directly results in our eternal position.

The reaction of the other 10 disciples is intriguing. They were greatly displeased with James and John. I know this is cynical, but I have always thought they were upset only because none of them had thought of it first. Every one of them secretly wondered what they were going to get out of this kind of life. Their reaction typifies one of the many dynamics of peer pressure.

We can only imagine the group dynamics among these 12 rustic, earthly, crude fishermen. Their lives together would have been "almost anything goes." In the midst of these group dynamics, Jesus was working to mature these men as individuals, as well as a group working together. He knew when he went back to heaven; the gospel would be in their hands. I wonder how many times Jesus felt that he wasn't getting through to them.

Peer pressure is the greatest source of personal failure, more than anything else. The fear of rejection and the need to be needed are the two things which create the greatest distress within the lives of millions. Succumbing to peer pressure seemingly meets these needs. The sad truth is, it is only a temporary solution. Succumbing to peer pressure makes the matters that concern you the most, much, much worse. The greatest thing each of us can do concerning peer pressure is to blaze our own path and leave a trail.

Jesus goes on to tell us all the answer to the spirit of pride, the spirit of power, and of peer pressure. It isn't anything close to natural, but will take care of the problems that beset each of us:

# We must be servants.

Jesus admonishes us that to be our greatest; we must first be the servant or slave of all. It is very interesting to note that Jesus never said it was wrong to want to be the greatest. We have drives and desires. God created us this way. Now Jesus is willing to help us channel and redirect our drives and desires. He insists that we focus all of our energy into meeting the needs of others first. This is a truth that can change lives. For example, going into a men's clothing store I am generally asked, "May I help you?" I always wonder if they really mean that. Recently a local men's store had a July half-price sale on selected suits. I went in the store to check out the bargains and immediately was engaged by a salesman. Before long this aggressive young man had five suits picked out for me. I liked them all. It was a great deal. But even at half price, the bill would have been $1450. There was no way I could have afforded it. Yet, despite my insistence that I was only considering one new suit, this young man continued to banter me about not being able to "afford" to pass up a great deal. Whose needs would be met here? Mine? Buying five suits for me, with a wife at home and raising two young boys, who constantly outgrow their clothes, did not seem right. Were we meeting his needs? Well — there you have it! Commission! He gave absolutely no thought to my financial condition. The servant meets the needs of others first and foremost.

I knew a chiropractor that often remarked, "Money is the product of services rendered." He felt that if he served others, the money would follow. I have found it usually does.

Overcoming the spirit of pride, the spirit of power and the spirit of peer pressure are possible only as we put others first by meeting their needs. We must consider ourselves slaves. Our attitudes must be one of serving and being a servant. If we apply these concepts, we will never be hell bent!

# CHAPTER 8

## "A HELL OF A DECEPTION!"

*"When Jesus came to the region of Caesarea Philippi,
he asked his disciples, 'Who do people say the Son of
Man is?' They replied, 'Some say John the Baptist;
others say Elijah; and still others, Jeremiah or one of
the prophets.' 'But what about you?' he asked. 'Who
do you say I am?' Simon Peter answered, 'You are the
Christ, the Son of the living God.' Jesus replied,
'Blessed are you, Simon son of Jonah, for this was not
revealed to you by man, but by my Father in heaven.
And I tell you that you are Peter, and on this rock I
will build my church, and the gates of Hades will not
overcome it. I will give you the keys of the kingdom of
heaven; whatever you bind on earth will be bound in
heaven, and whatever you loose on earth will be
loosed in heaven.' Then he warned his disciples not to
tell anyone that he was the Christ."* — *Matthew
16:13-20*

Have you ever studied something to determine the truth, only
to become frustrated? Many times it is extremely difficult to
find the real from the fake. Deception is an obviously
apparent element today. It creates an atmosphere whereby
one never knows, or can only discover through careful
scrutiny, what is true and what is false.

To illustrate — antique auctions can be one of these places
of deception. I had a friend who was an auctioneer.
Fortunately, he was also an expert on antiques. Many, many
times people would try to pass off a fake as a valuable,
authentic antique. This happened continually with
glassware, furniture, coins and equipment. He had to
become an expert quickly and not disclose his expertise to
anyone. Really, his role of auctioneer of antiques was as

close to Jesus' admonition to "be as wise as serpents and harmless as doves" as any I have ever seen.

More than just antiques; deception is present in most every situation in our world today. It is not obvious, visible, or apparent, yet it is still apparent today.

Deception is an important issue when dealing with Hell. The essence of evil is to pry, drag, pull and move people toward its influence.

I had a broadcasting friend who would often laugh about Christians who blamed the devil for their behavior. He saw Christians who blamed the devil as people who copped out of their own responsibilities.

Deception is the link for which we are looking. It is that space of blame between the issue of "who is at fault?" We make mistakes in our lives because we become deceived. When leasing a car became the "in" thing, I leased one. What looked like a great deal for me, really was not. Many of the things the dealer said about leasing a car were not true. Many of his promises were never backed up. The lease I signed had many contingencies that it left up to the dealer. When it came time to make a change, the dealer looked out for himself.

Many would say I messed up because I didn't have all the promises in writing. That is right. What I heard and what actually were the facts in writing was not the same.

There are many other kinds of deceptions. Reading maps, campaign speeches, advertising, taxes, automobile deals, are all just a very few of the many ways we become deceived on a day-to-day basis.

Have you ever joined a record or book club to get five items for a dollar with the promise of future great deals? After your initial items are worn out, you still have to buy a book or record a month for 24 months. It is the shipping and handling charge that is always so outrageous. Deception is present in all of our lives, every day of our lives!

On and on we could go about how often we are faced with deception, but we must face an important truth: God **still holds us responsible for our choices!** They say the law about taxes is "Ignorance is no excuse!" In other words, just because you were not aware of a particular tax law, you are not innocent if you violate that particular tax law. The same is true about deception. God gives us all the truth we need to keep from being deceived. The problem occurs when we make mistakes and can't see through the deception that is present. Even though we did not catch the deception, we are still responsible.

It does not matter what your personal theology is at this point, as long as you can accept the fact that deception comes from hell. Deception is the essence of the evil realm. The most physically beautiful things in life can actually do us the greatest harm. The old saying, "Looks are deceiving" has never been truer.

If God really does hold us responsible for deception, whether we see it or not, there must be some things we can do to improve ourselves. There are some things we can do! Before we can begin to apply them, we must firmly believe that all forms of deception are our mortal enemies. We must see deception as the outreach event of hell. It wants to pull us in and suck us into hell with it. This may sound like a violent approach, but it is a necessary thought pattern for overcoming deception.

Matthew 16:13-20 gives us some ideas and a model in its dialogue for avoiding deception. When applied to our day-to-day lives, the results can be extremely helpful. This passage is Jesus' discussion with his disciples concerning who he was to others, as well as to his disciples. What a fine passage to develop this model! Its core of meaning is who

Jesus was — which is really what all other discussions of deception stem from. Jesus Christ is the standard by which the Christian judges all other things. Hell itself flees from Jesus to the "nth" degree. All truth flows toward the Son of Man. The Son of Man repels all falsity. It is from this point; that we develop principles to avoid deception.

## PRINCIPLES TO AVOID DECEPTION

### Get a sense of what the world says.

Jesus asked the disciples point blank, "Who do men say I am?" He knew they had heard. Now he was asking them to admit it. This is not to say we should delve into worldliness. We don't have to delve into it to know what it says. Jesus said in another place to "be in the world, but not of it." This is the essence of this first principle.

Christians should not take pride in being innocent or sheltered. It is only through weathering the storms of life that we become stronger and wiser. This concept may cause us to fear, since we have spent many decades trying to tell people they must make the appearance to the world of being "set apart." If we fall into this trap of appearances, and really don't feel "set apart" in our hearts, we are as deceptive internally as the deception we are trying to avoid. It is not good, then, to be stupid about the world. We need to keep our ears and eyes open, and our mouths shut. Getting a sense of where the world is coming from will help you catch the sense of how Jesus can save that same world. He just might use you to be a facilitator to do just that.

### Know what you believe.

Jesus' next question to his disciples was, "Who do you say that I am?" This was again another point blank question. This drew his disciples close to him. If Jesus had been anyone else but the Son of Man, he would have braced his ego for the worst. He wasn't an ordinary man. He was the God/man. Their response was their own conviction. He wanted desperately for these men to have their own belief system. He trained them and taught them, but the choice of values was their own.

Spending day and night for three years with Jesus would have had an impact on each of them. Yet their soul-felt values would come from their own beliefs. Their job was to correlate all Christ said with how they felt, and apply it to life, then take that outcome and reflect upon it. Then they would need to reapply it along with other input. On and on the cycle goes, creating a belief system within each of us.

Our belief systems are very personal, but they are not private, for they are obvious in our daily living. We may not dogmatically proclaim our belief systems, but it is who and what we are on a daily, personal level. These systems of belief vary with each individual. No two people are identical. As different as personalities are, so are belief systems. Don't let this scare you. Even people going to the same church can have different belief systems. Jesus never tried to create robots. What He tries to create are individuals with their belief systems carefully worked out through the course of life.

The most important thing is to know what you personally believe. Work it out in your daily life. Each of us must. We can't say we believe something just because someone tells us to, or he or she believes it, until we have personally worked it out. We often believe something because our parents do, but until we personally work it out, it is not really our own belief system.

I remember being in grade school during a presidential election. My fourth grade teacher talked extensively about the election, as well as the candidates. She insisted that none of us comment about the candidates. She said that by doing so, we would reveal our parent's political party, which was a personal issue. As fourth graders, I think we resented her approach, but she was right. We were not old enough yet to develop our own belief systems about our politics.

The strife of the 1960's brought about discontent and, at times, bloodshed. Rebellion was in the air. Things went too far. If we could simply give people the space to work through what they believe, we could save the bloodshed. But we must know what we believe. What do you believe?

**The Belief System Cycle.**

> **Application of Value/Belief: Reflection of Input**

> **Strength of Conviction: Testing of Application of Value-Belief Input**

> **Teachableness in Life: A Life Event**

Develop a clear sense of Jesus' place in your life; this will affect your perspective on everything.

Jesus' constant inference with regard to himself and the involvement of others was "all or nothing!" This makes Jesus a total, complete, radical!

Simon Peter answered Jesus' question *of "Who do you say that I am?"* very clearly. He said, *"Thou art the Christ, the Son of the living God."* Simon Peter answered Jesus' question with absolute clarity, deep from within his soul.

The relevance of Simon Peter's answer is in its conviction of truth. Every perspective Simon Peter had would flow out of this one conviction. Everything he looked at and how he looked at it, was under the scope of who Jesus was. Who Jesus was affected everything else in his life.

This third principle of avoiding deception is clearly the most important principle. It is not nearly so important that we absolutely adopt Simon Peter's perspective, as much as it is that we develop our own answer to Jesus' question. We then must allow our answer to be our central perspective in life.

Developing a clear sense of Jesus' place in your life requires three things:

1. **An acceptance of His invitation to be a personal part of your life**. This happens as a result of our admission of our lost state, and our openness to His plan of redemption for us.

2. **A submission to His authority.** His authority is found in His Word. This indicates our willingness to form a personal relationship with Him.

3. **An openness to His direction.** The personal relationship with Jesus is a growing, building one. Our openness to Him gives us the ability to grow, adapt, and strive for a better life and richer freedoms.

**Gain Your Own Personal Revelation.**

Does this sound cult-like in its word structure? It is meant to sound that way because this is the way cults are started. Deception runs rampant. When everyone gets their own personal revelations and begin to spew them out, they develop their own followings.

When Simon Peter answered Jesus, he answered so sincerely and completely, that Jesus responded with a remark that has often been misinterpreted. The emphasis has been placed on Simon Peter's known name, "Petra." We will look at this in a later principle all its own. The real emphasis should be placed upon who revealed the true answer to Peter. Jesus said it wasn't "flesh and blood", but instead "my Father which is in heaven."

The point is, Jesus will build the future of the world upon the Father's revelations to individuals. Jesus is, in fact, ushering in the advent of the Holy Spirit. He is doing some concentrated teaching about the church age.

The points to be made from here should not be <u>does</u> God speak, but <u>how</u> He speaks. Jesus made it clear in the text that God does speak and reveals Himself. He also <u>wants</u> to speak and reveal Himself.

The question is how does God speak and reveal Himself? The answer is through His Word by the Holy Spirit!

The personal revelation of God to man comes through the Holy Spirit by way of personal Bible study. I know this sounds simple compared to the sound of the principle. The biggest reason deception is so present is because Christians just don't know God's Word. If they do, they lack the personal relationship with Jesus through the Holy Spirit. This relationship takes the words of the Bible and applies them to everyday, personal areas of life.

As one develops this "personal" revelation, all forms of deception will be revealed.

## Go Rock Hunting!

This fifth principle may sound trite, but it is really very powerful. The Scriptures, and especially Jesus' teachings, speak much of building. The strength and endurance of the building is seen in its foundation. The rock foundation in the near-eastern culture was the symbol of stability. That is the exact point of this principle. If we build our lives upon stability, we won't be easily deceived!

This is not to say we will never be deceived, but it is more difficult to be deceived when one's attitude and actions take on more stability. There are three things you must do to achieve stability:

1. **Do not allow your attitudes to swing heavily in any direction.** Negativity creates great discontent and makes a person very unsettled. The same is true of a hyper-positive attitude. When your attitude is hyper, you are alone and all by yourself. People don't want to have anything to do with you. Try to achieve a moderate and optimistic attitude consistently.

2. **Be moderate in all things.** This is not an original idea by any means. Moderation is an important key to achieving stability in life. If you consistently let go and don't say no, an addictive type behavior can actually develop. An addict is the most unstable person in the world. Moderation in all things helps us to avoid mood swings and many behavioral problems.

3. **Develop balance.** Balance sounds similar to moderation, but it requires different dynamics. Balance requires the help of those closest to you. Being able to interact and debrief your behavior with others is the key to leading a balanced life. To do this, one must be able to trust others and listen to their input.

Stability is an important principle, not just in reference to avoiding deception, but in consistent successes in our lives!

## Understand the Importance of the Course of Life!

This sixth principle of avoiding deception has to do with Jesus' pronouncement, "build my church."

The idea of "build" means to construct and confirm. This was always God's idea for our lives. Even in the Garden of Eden, God told Adam to go forth, replenish, and subdue the earth. God's intention has always been for us to glorify Him through our efforts. Our efforts are to be building blocks.

Each day is supposed to have meaning; every thought, word, action, and attitude are to have a great effect upon our own lives today, and also for our eternal life.

Jesus' word, "church" (ekklesai in the original language) means more than just the community of believers. It means the unseen heavenly realm as well. The importance of the lifestyle of the believer and the application each makes of Biblical principles cannot be too carefully mentioned. It is not too intense to say that even the slightest error can change things for all eternity. Conversely, the good work of the Spirit-led believer can change all things for eternity as well. It will be quite a day when we see things as they are and not how they seem.

The way I feel about the intensity of this concept would be extremely difficult to communicate except for a recent TV program I saw called, "Quantum Leap". The program was a drama based upon quantum physics. A man travels through time-changing situations which affect a chain of situations on and on through time. Appearing with this time traveler is what they call a "hologram" which communicates to him his mission and what happens if he doesn't succeed.

The TV show displays how one event can change the course of history. We must understand how the same is true in each of our own lives. Don't underestimate even one small decision. The careful attention one gives to every detail will help tremendously to wipe out any possible deception.

**Be an Overcomer by Being Attentive.**

The final principle in avoiding deception is to pay attention! Jesus said, *"and the gates of hell shall not prevail against it."*

From the text, it is apparent that hell is not satisfied with sitting by and watching things happen. The power of evil is a constant pressure in all of our lives.

As much pressure we receive, there is a greater power within every Christian believer to overcome it. The power to overcome is simply the ability to let Jesus have control and reign in every area of our lives. The more one feeds something, the bigger it will grow. This is true of both good and evil. The force of evil does not have to overpower you, if you will simply be attentive.

Being attentive requires three very important things. These are not new, but they serve as a reminder of what it takes to overcome whatever the "gates of hell" will throw our way:

1. **Be alert**. Keeping your eyes open to the wiles of the devil is critical. The idea of alertness is seen in the Scripture, *"Be sober, be vigilant; because your adversary the devil, as a roaming lion, walketh about, seeking whom he may devour."* I Peter 5:8

   I have often said that Satan, being a created being, cannot read our minds. If this is true, then our alertness is really learning that we need to keep our mouths shut. Satan can plant our minds with thoughts, but he only knows when he has gotten through to us by our words and actions. If we hear a thought, but don't act upon it, Satan does not know he has gotten through. Allow this concept to help you become alert.

2. **Be consistent**. Alertness is created by consistency. I believe the greatest problem in the Church, as a whole, is inconsistency. When we are inconsistent, we hurt any good we have done. Being up and down, in and out is the roller-coaster type of existence many Christians live spiritually. No wonder they are

deceived by the devil, because they are taken in by every imaginable cause or soapbox. Inconsistent people are those who are all go when they are up, but you never see them when they are down. When they are up, they have every kind of advice and counsel on how to do things better. The only way to build the Kingdom of Heaven is through constant, consistent effort.

3. **Be committed.** Commitment is the ability within the brain to absolutely resolve to follow through with something. Commitment is the key to success in anything. The more committed one is, the better one does.

# CHAPTER 9

## "GOING TO HELL IN A HANDBASKET"

I have watched it happen too many times, people slipping away spiritually.

His name was Terry and he was my Sunday school teacher in the fourth grade. He was short, but extremely powerful. He had been a weight lifter and had an imposing physique. Terry had belonged to a motorcycle gang before he was saved. He was mean, vulgar, and carried a gun in those days before his conversion. His father had left his mother with four kids to raise, at a very young age. Terry became bitter toward the father he never knew, and rebellious toward his mother who tried desperately to raise him. Through various circumstances, Terry ran with the wrong crowd. Nothing was too immoral, too filthy, too evil, too dirty, or too wicked for him to do.

One day someone witnessed to Terry. For the first time in his 20 years, he heard about Jesus and a savior who loved him. Through that simple testimony, this burley, rebellious, mean young man got saved. Soon after, his wife got saved. Shortly after that, they started coming to church.

Terry fully submerged himself in church activities. He wanted to do everything. Many around him were afraid he would get burned out, but that never concerned him. He was now giving God the time he had previously given the motorcycle gang.

I run into people, all the time that complain about church involvement, yet give their time to many selfish activities. Terry threw himself into the church. He wanted to be in and around the church every day.

On Sundays, he taught the fourth grade class, sang in the choir, served as an usher, and greeted people at the door. On

Mondays, he led the follow-up on first time visitors. On Tuesday, he had a deacon's meeting. On Wednesdays, he led the youth group. On Thursdays, he led a group of people around neighborhoods to canvass for bus ministry. On Fridays, he was the director of family night at the gym. Saturdays were workday, followed by nursing home services.

In addition to all of this, Terry's old friends were coming to church — and to the Lord — through Terry's influence. This was an interesting thing to watch, since Terry's friends would come with their motorcycle gang jackets on, blue jeans, t-shirts, long, matted hair and beards. There were many, many raised eyebrows in those days.

Terry kept this pace for five years, and then things started to happen. He started to mention little cynical things about church people in a humorous way. Then once in a while he would be critical of the pastor behind his back. Soon he was resigning his ministries for this reason or that reason. Eventually, over the course of two more years, he became inconsistent with my class. They would either find a last minute substitute who hadn't prepared, or combine us with a lower grade. Once or twice, we didn't have a Sunday school teacher and no one checked on us. There we were — five fourth graders in a Sunday school class alone for an hour.

Eventually people began to notice Terry dropping out of the services he once attended. Then mysteriously his employer wanted him to work every other Sunday. This had never happened before because he wouldn't let it. Many times he testified in church about his employer and witnessing to him. Now he was slipping away.

Just a very few of God's precious people confronted Terry. He was always defensive and offended when anyone questioned him.

One time he even forbade his family to come to church because "they are all hypocrites trying to run our life."

As I write this story, I am very saddened. The rough draft of this manuscript has tearstains on it. Despite the difficulty I have talking about my friend Terry, we must face this area in our study on hell. It is one of the elements of hell I call degeneration. Degeneration occurs as the once growing Christian believer becomes overcome with the sense of self and degenerates spiritually. It is ugly and awful, but we must face it. We must be realistic and learn the steps to avoid spiritual degeneration.

Terry's story only gets worse. At that time in his life, he was 27 and had two small children. He worked days and his wife worked nights. Because of an overlap in schedules, they had a live-in, 17-year-old babysitter. Because of Terry's degenerative spiritual state, the babysitter and Terry developed an ongoing affair. Terry finally ran off with the babysitter one day, leaving his small children in their beds while his wife was at work. He packed his clothes and left her a note. He never went back.

Some years later I felt led to go see him. I found him in a back alley up some steps in a one-room apartment. A girl of about 15 answered the door. She went to get Terry. He came to the door, never asking me in. The conversation was distant. I told him of my plans to enter the ministry. I spoke to him of the influence he had on my life as a boy in Sunday school. He was cold. He looked old. He couldn't have been 35, but looked 60. I could tell he was uncomfortable with me there. Terry looked like hell — literally.

I asked him about his soul and he confidently told me of his great spiritual life he had with just him and God. He was deceived and misled. Yet, he knew just the right words to say. From all of his church years, he learned the vocabulary we use. He had picked up the lingo to get Christians off his back.

The degeneration I have described is all too common. It is happening to many Christians in every city, in every church, in every family — every day.

As I left Terry that last day I saw him, I resolved to do anything within my power to stop spiritual degeneration. There is a scriptural passage in Psalm 9 that gives me my message for degeneration. It shows us in verse 17, *"The wicked are turned into hell"*. This is in the King James Version. The NIV says, *"The wicked are turned into the grave."* This verse is in no way a lesson in Calvinism or Armenism.

The arguments of these dogmas should not be a factor. In fact, I have always felt that part of the reason for degeneration is that Christians have spent far too much time discussing and arguing over dogmas, instead of directing people spiritually. "Hell" or "grave" is the concept of misery. The whole point of this book on hell is to show there is a miserable place of hell to shun.

Degeneration is hell. My friend Terry was a miserable person who could not seem to pull himself out of the degenerative, downward spiral he was in. Psalm 9 is our answer! We must heed it and make it personal, lest the rest of us fall into degeneration as well. We each must be on guard against the degenerative spirit. We must apply the four truths found in this passage. It must become part of our lives. Tell it to your friends. Tell it to your children. Tell it to everyone!

*"Sing praises to the LORD, enthroned in Zion; proclaim among the nations what he has done. For he who avenges blood remembers; he does not ignore the cry of the afflicted. O LORD, see how my enemies*

*persecute me! Have mercy and lift me up from the gates of death, that I may declare your praises in the gates of the Daughter of Zion and there rejoice in your salvation. The nations have fallen into the pit they have dug; their feet are caught in the net they have hidden. The LORD is known by his justice; the wicked are ensnared by the work of their hands. The wicked return to the grave, all the nations that forget God. But the needy will not always be forgotten, nor the hope of the afflicted ever perish. Arise, O LORD, let not man triumph; let the nations be judged in your presence. Strike them with terror, O LORD; let the nations know they are but men."  — Psalms 9:11-20*

## SING PRAISES v. 11

The Bible and psychology books have much to say about being happy. We need to laugh. We need to loosen up. We need to be happy.

Degeneration usually takes the track of a more cynical, negative mentality. If we could learn how to change this mentality permanently, we could learn to isolate and wipe out the degenerative spirit. The first truth to overcoming degeneration is to "sing praises."

Rather than walk around your home, work, or school, beating out hymns and Christian choruses, we need to take this Scriptural point found in verse 11 and make it work in our lives. There are two things to do to get yourself on the right track to singing praises:

1. Your attitude affects any outcome. Notice the word is <u>affect</u> not effect. The difference between these two words in this context is that effect watches things happen whereas <u>affect</u> makes things happen. More specifically, please understand there is nothing mystical about this, our attitudes have nothing to do

with the factors and elements that bring us an outcome. However, once an outcome has happened, then how we accept it, apply it, and synthesize it into our lives is how it "affects" us. The bottom line of this truth is we can allow an outcome to affect us any way we want it to. The decision on how something affects us is up to us. It is contingent upon our attitude.

2. Count your blessings! The second way to sing praises is to constantly be counting our blessings in life. Name them out loud one by one. This is such an excellent thought. Sometimes we are so into pity, which is a sign of degeneration, that we can't even get started counting. Start with your salvation, as seen in verse 14. Remember that all of us have good things happen. We all have bad things happen. What we dwell on most will determine our countenance!

These two things are an imperative in singing praises and thereby applying this first truth of overcoming degeneration.

## DECLARE HIS DOING AMONG THE PEOPLE v. 11

The second truth goes like this. Degeneration sets in when a person no longer declares the good things God is doing in the lives of people. This is not to say just in one's own life, but in the lives of everyone. As a matter of fact, when one always tells of the good things God does in one's own life without mentioning others, it can get fairly lopsided and selfish.

God is constantly doing good things in the lives of people. We must be very quick to proclaim it to everyone everywhere.

People have a tendency to talk about the things that interest them the most. When you hook up with a person in dialogue, they will soon talk about the thing or things that mean the most to them. How often do you hear conversations about God? Here is a tougher question even closer to home: How often do you hear Christian talk about God in their conversations? What you talk about the most is of the greatest importance to you!

I read Joe Girard's book "How to Sell Anything to Anyone". In it Joe has a very intriguing theory he calls Girard's law of 155. He believes that everyone in the world has a sphere of influence of 155 people. Each of us is able to influence to some degree or another or various degrees up to 155 people. His point is if you offended even one person, you are in fact offending their whole world of 155 people.

In this second truth in overcoming degeneration, I want to use his principle in a new way. Each of us has our own world we are able to influence. The number of people in our sphere of influence is not nearly as important as our type of influence. We have a world in each of our lives to declare His doings to. If someone is excited about something, they will tell others about it. They will tell others in direct proportion to their excitement. There is nothing that will break the back of the degenerative spirit like declaring God's doings among the people!

## DON'T COMPLAIN v. 13

This third truth for overcoming degeneration comes from the 13th verse, *"Have mercy upon me, O Lord, consider my trouble, which I suffer of them that hate me, thou that lifteth me up from the gates of death."*

This point may be better put, "suffer silently" as the verse says. The phrase, "don't complain" broadens it enough to include all of us.

Many times when we go through hardships, we feel like God has forgotten about us. Things create an atmosphere in our hearts of self-pity. Self-pity is the start of a very unfortunate degenerating spiritual sayonara. This sayonara may include resentment, then bitterness, then rebellion, and then disfellowship from God. This is an ugly turn of events that could be avoided if it were nipped in the bud. The way to avoid it is by resolving to not complain. If we decide not to be a complainer, we then avoid criticalness, pickiness, and shallowness. There are so many things that make life worse which can be avoided if we would simply decide to not be a complainer.

Complaining gets us absolutely nowhere. Even if it appears to help with a few changes, it is only in the temporal. Changes that truly make a difference need to occur in the eternal sense. The way to see these changes is not through complaining, but through prayer. If we look to people for comfort, help or to change the situation, we will generally be disappointed and hence create a degenerative spirit. At the very least we will create an atmosphere for degeneration spiritually.

The only answer we have is to stop complaining and spend time alone with God. Talking, communing, sharing, fasting, and praying to God is the answer. The person who does these things and suffers silently will not only have a better peace of mind, and can be closer to God, but will cut off the degenerative spirit which sends people to hell!

## BECOME NEEDY v. 18

We have saved the hardest for last! Verse 18 says, "For the needy shall not always be forgotten." One very evident characteristic of the person, who is degenerating spiritually is his spirit of independence. It is marked by an obvious sense of self-sufficiency. A person who is degenerative spiritually generally always contends everything is well with his soul. This contention comes off defensive. It really is defensiveness, but it is often coming from a person who is trying to justify his behavior to himself.. This type of person is extremely difficult to get through to.

The lesson to be learned is that to overcome degeneration, we must stay in a constant state of need. It is our dependency upon God through neediness which keeps us as close as we should be to Him.

The toughest prayer anyone could pray is, "Lord, make me needy." We are afraid of this prayer because we really don't know what needs He may bring. Growing Christians can be recognized by their self-professed needs.

Whenever you feel like you can make it on your own; or you don't need any help; or your needs are covered; then examine your soul quickly — degeneration is setting in!

## AND FINALLY — TERROR

The final verse says, "Strike them with terror, O Lord; let the nations know they are but men." (Ps. 9:20)

The greatest terror in life is to lose a loved one. It forces us to face our own mortality. It forces us to confront God. The Psalmist's final words are a prayer for all of us to come to God. This prayer is for those who are degenerating to come to their senses.

Never is it so aptly illustrated than at the funeral of a young person. Young people do die, but until death occurs to a friend, one may never think about his life or the life hereafter.

I received an emergency page at a teen camp I was directing. My wife was crying when I returned the call. At first I thought something had happened to one of our sons.

Instead, she gave me the news that one of our 18 year old boys in our church had just been killed when his jack kicked out from under the bumper of his Mustang. He was changing his oil and the oil pan crushed his chest. They say he died slowly.

The night of the visitation and the funeral were the epitome of emotion. He was in the peak of health and vitality. He was the star fullback of the high school football team. Hundreds of young people came to grieve. Their shock was apparent. They each were coming face to face with their own mortality. It terrorized them. I will never forget their faces.

I will also never forget the thought that crossed my mind. God will stop at nothing to arrest the spirit of degeneration. He will literally do anything or pay any price. He would even give up His own Son. And that is exactly what he did.

Overcome degeneration in your own life and preach the four truths to overcoming degeneration from Psalm 9 to the world!

Heeding these warnings simply will determine our ultimate spiritual and eternal destination!

# CHAPTER 10

## "A LIFE OF HELL!"

Have you ever felt trapped? Feeling trapped is literally hell to most people. They live through it, they feel it, they experience it, and the more they try to get free, the worse it gets. The feeling of being trapped reminds me of a vise that gets tighter and tighter. A couple of years ago, my oldest son broke his arm. It was a double break. When the orthopedic surgeon came in, he said he was going to set it with the cast. He wetted down the materials and wrapped them around his little arm. My son held his arm perfectly still ten minutes. As the cast dried, he screamed in pain. This pain was a result of the materials realigning the broken bones naturally.

Being and feeling trapped brings out the same pain. When you feel trapped, you feel like there is no way out. Several years ago I had a man in my church named Dan. Over several weeks, his complexion began to turn white, then gray, and then ashen. It was obvious Dan was becoming sick and dying or something was acutely affecting his life.

One day I went out to his house. It was an old farmhouse, very modest by many standards. This house and the 20 acres it was on had been in the family for four generations. His father was born, raised, and died in that home. Dan was born in the same room in which his father and grandfather had died. They were simple people with modest tastes and little education. Sitting in the kitchen around that 100-year-old round oak table, I heard his sad cry at the conflict. After his father had died, the 40 acres next to their 20 acres went up for sale. It was in the days when farmers bought all the land they could get their hands on. Land was escalating so in price that it seemed there would never be an end to what it would be worth. Dan mortgaged the free and clear 20 acre homestead to buy the additional 40 acres. Then the bottom dropped out of the market. He lost his job. The bank was foreclosing. He was losing his family homestead, which had been clear of debt since 1915. It was his fault, and it was literally killing this 35-year-old man physically. He was going through a life of hell!

Dan's story does not have a pretty ending. His family homestead was sold at a sheriff's land bankruptcy sale. The new owner bulldozed his home down.

The real clincher is Dan and his family made it through. They have a nice little home in town now. They both work and are raising three boys.

Dan's story is not unusual. The feeling of being trapped affects people we come into contact with all day long. Scripture speaks of these feelings in many places:

> *"The cords of the grave coiled around me; the snares of death confronted me."* — *2 Samuel 22:6*

Psalm 18:5 speaks of the prevalent sorrows of hell. The pain of hell is seen in Psalm 116:3 and Psalm 55:15. Psalm 16:10 says, *"My soul is turned into hell."* Psalm 139:8 says, *"Make a bed for me in hell."*

In this chapter of our look at hell, we want to specifically look at the feeling of being trapped. In the next chapter we will look at going through hell. The most notable figure in the Bible who gives us a colorful illustration of being and feeling trapped is Jonah in the belly of the whale. Jonah's prayer in chapter 2:1-10 is a classic. It gives us a look at Jonah's soul. He clearly presents his feelings. We see the case he makes to God. But in the end, we see that God delivered him only after he fully learned the lesson of his entrapment. Yes, we are going to be quite philosophical about this feeling of being trapped and the subsequent "life of hell!"

*"From inside the fish Jonah prayed to the LORD his God. He said: 'In my distress I called to the LORD, and he answered me. From the depths of the grave I called for help, and you listened to my cry. You hurled me into the deep, into the very heart of the seas, and the currents swirled about me; all your waves and breakers swept over me. I said, 'I have been banished from your sight; yet I will look again toward your holy temple.' The engulfing waters threatened me, the deep surrounded me; seaweed was wrapped around my head. To the roots of the mountains I sank down; the earth beneath barred me in forever. But you brought my life up from the pit, O LORD my God. When my life was ebbing away, I remembered you, LORD, and my prayer rose to you, to your holy temple. Those who cling to worthless idols forfeit the grace that could be theirs. But I, with a song of thanksgiving, will sacrifice to you. What I have vowed I will make good. Salvation comes from the LORD.' And the LORD commanded the fish, and it vomited Jonah onto dry land."*
*— Jonah 2*

The Lord provided a great fish to swallow Jonah. There is really no indication of how long it was between the time he was thrown overboard, and the time the fish swallowed him. Every time I read Jonah's prayer, I am convinced Jonah thought he was dead.

It is dreadful to bring it up while thinking of Jonah drowning, but I have always pictured the cartoons here. When I was a kid, whenever anyone was drowning, they would go down three times. Each time they went under they would hold up a finger. One the first, two the second, and three for the final time. After the third finger, they were a goner! This is how I picture Jonah — down for the final time.

Sometime during this gruesome scene comes a whale to snatch him up. I've never been inside the belly of a whale and can only imagine it. My imagination runs away with itself, only in the most awful direction. Inside the belly of the whale it was pitch dark. Surgeons say that the digestive juices of the human stomach contain elements that can break and digest anything naturally produced. If you have ever vomited, you know in a small measure the smell and substance which completely engulfed Jonah. Jonah himself was probably tossed to and fro by the stomach muscles which would be treating him as an unwanted intruder. The natural reaction of Jonah's presence in the whale's stomach would probably have caused the stomach to release bile and digestive juices in great quantities to break him down.

It is this touch of hell in Jonah's life that we will analyze. There are nine lessons to be learned. We don't have to be overcome by the feeling of being trapped. These nine things will create a great model to overcome the feeling of being trapped.

First, **without the fish, Jonah would be dead**. When the waves and water engulfed him, he thought he was dead. The fish was the thing God chose to use to give Jonah an intermission from life and learn a lesson. Many times we find ourselves in situations which are unbecoming and uncomfortable. Most of the time we carry on and complain as if there is no God and there is no tomorrow. Yet, in the midst of our griping, God has put us right where we are to preserve us long enough to teach us a lesson.

Without the fish, Jonah would be dead! Your feeling of entrapment that you may be experiencing right now is your big fish. Believe it or not, it has been sent to preserve your life. Whatever your feeling of being trapped is, the best way to handle it is to actually view it as preservation. The feeling of being trapped actually works like the nerves in our bodies.

No one likes to feel pain, but pain is necessary to send us the message that something is wrong in our bodies.

I have a very good friend who is paralyzed from the chest down. Last year, he started to have kidney trouble, but didn't know it. He could feel no pain. There was no warning sign to him. We just noticed the change in his color and energy level. It started to worry us all until he had some surgery to correct the problem. In the same way, our emotions and feelings are not our enemies. They indicate to us many different things. The feeling of being trapped is not really the hell that we have actually thought. If we look at it in this light, feeling trapped becomes the fish sent by God, rather than the killer whale wanting to devour us!

Second, **Jonah was in the belly of the whale because he left the center of God's will**. This is something we often forget to consider. God told Jonah to go to Ninevah, but he did not want to go. The men threw him off the side of the ship because they perceived, and rightfully so, that he was the cause of their turbulence. This all happened because Jonah did not listen to God. He was out of God's will for his life.

God generally gets the brunt of all our mistakes. We ignore His commands and guidelines. We blame Him then when our lives don't turn out the way we planned.

Yesterday, on the way out the door of church, a lady handed me a note. In it she wrote of how her two sons didn't want to come to church. Her explanation to them was that God and the church were their only hope. The older one said, "What has God ever done for us?" She revealed in her note that she felt the same way. Her so-called husband was threatening her physically, etc. She feels trapped and blames God. That is what she sees and feels. The fact is the man whom she lives with is not her husband. The man who is her husband does not want a divorce. She is living in adultery openly before her sons, and is expecting God to heal her relationship with her boyfriend. She wrote in her note that her life seemed like a "prison." She continued on with the fact that she feels trapped because she is totally dependent upon the man for income. That is why she does not move out. This "life of hell" of hers and the feeling of being trapped are not God's fault at all. She wants God to go against his own commandments to help her. She is feeling trapped because she is completely out of the center of God's will.

I have heard many renditions of knowing God's will. Many people make knowing God's will a big concern. The truth is as long as we obey God's Word; his will is revealed to us, as we need it, a step at a time. God's will is not hard to find.

Maybe you are in the belly of the whale and feeling trapped, but want to find God's will again. We will look at that later.

Third, **it was so dark, Jonah might not have known where he was.** He might have actually thought he was dead. He might have thought he was in hell. Dark, smelly, bursts of movement, foreign sounds, these would have been things unimaginable.

A whale has many chambers in its stomach. It takes a long time for food to digest. In fact, a whale's stomach will pass food back and forth many times through its chambers before it is digested.

There are times when our emotions drop into the pit of despair as well. During these times, we might even lose track of where we are. This might sound a little unbelievable, but mental institutions are full of people who simply lost touch with their identity. It is purely mental, wrought through emotions.

Losing track of where you are is brought on by both the feelings of being trapped, as well as propitiating the feeling of being trapped. Jonah was in the belly of the whale and the darkness was actually closing in on him. Knowing where we are at in all situations and at all times is an imperative. It simply is the only way we can survive. If this does not seem possible, we must learn the fourth lesson.

Fourthly, **Jonah shows us that in the deepest pits, God is our only hope of deliverance.** This is not something that will automatically come, nor will it naturally come. It is a thought that has to be so believed; it goes clear down deep into the soul to the point it will come back to you when needed.

An interesting thing happened several years ago. A man started coming to my church who was a farmer. He was a younger man of 35 years of age and had inherited 200 acres from his deceased father. Much like the man we mentioned earlier, Fred mortgaged what he had to buy the land next to him (about 400 acres). Fred seemed to be doing well financially. However, one day I heard that Fred was in trouble. I went out to call on him and found out that he was being indicted by a federal grand jury. I guess the reason Fred did so well financially was because he allowed his barn to be used by 18-wheelers full of dope. They parked these big rigs in Fred's barn to "cool off." Each truck full of dope was worth around $10,000,000. Fred made tens of thousands of dollars over four years' time.

The night I went out, be was trying to decide to cooperate with the FBI and DEA and plea bargain. To do so, he would have to "narc" on everyone he knew and tell everything. If he did so, he faced five years in a federal prison. If he didn't talk, he faced life in prison. If he did talk, he was risking his life every day for the rest of his life. The FBI and DEA were starting to bring down a drug ring, and nothing or no one was going to stand in their way.

I shared the gospel with Fred. He felt alone and trapped. What he did was illegal, immoral, and ruined the lives of young people. I believed he sincerely was repentant and felt bad. Yet, in the face of his life of hell, he could not throw his soul to the mercy of Jesus. He told me something that I felt was rather remarkable. Fred said that he wouldn't accept Jesus as his savior because that was what the man had done who turned him in to the FBI. Fred quoted the person as saying he was turning Fred's name over "for Jesus' sake." This left Fred bitter. Yet he told me he felt that I was sincere.

Time passed and Fred kept coming to church. At his arraignment, the bail was set at $100,000, which Fred could easily pay. Every day that went by, the more Fred felt trapped. One night in the darkest moments of his life, Fred turned to Jesus. Fred finally realized deep down in his soul that his only hope of deliverance was from God. Fred experienced saving faith. He told what he knew and got off with eight years of probation. He had to do plenty of community work as well. **God is our only hope of deliverance!**

Fifth, **when life is ebbing away, remember the Lord and raise your prayers.** This is exactly what Jonah did! Remembering the Lord is as simple as calling out to him at the time of need. Lifting a prayer is as easy as communicating to a loving father. To achieve these rather simple exercises to help us during those times of feeling trapped, we must realize that God desires to have a true parent-child relationship with each of us. Conceptualizing this kind of love will help us remember to tap into it when life seems like hell.

Another thing to realize is that it is never too late to cry out to God. We can never go too far in our failures that God will not hear us. No matter how trapped you feel, God is close enough to help you out of those troubled feelings. Unless one has this confidence, life is hopeless. With this confidence, life can be lifted up out of the pit.

A final point to realize is that it is only God who can restore your strength. Jonah spent three days and nights in the belly of the whale. He had no track of time. It would have been like an acute form of jet lag. He was so exhausted; he felt the life in his body leaving him. He thought he was dying. When you feel like this, God is the only one who can restore your energy!

Sixth, **we must bring down every idol!** Idols are anything which separate us from God. An idol is anything that comes between God and us. We could even say it is something that we love more than God.

The truth about the feeling of being trapped is, we generally have developed an idol which results in the emotional pit of feeling like life is hell. The problem is that we rarely, if ever, admit this is the case. We are so able to justify our own behavior that we become oblivious to the idea that our emotional pit has a spiritual problem as its root.

The idols people have are as different as are the individuals. Whatever is between you and God will eventually entrap you and make your life like hell. Many people have human relationships as their idols. One day Jesus' mother and family were waiting for him. They requested he come to them out of loyalty to them. Jesus made it quite clear that his love and loyalty were to God and his people. Many have allowed their human relationships to accelerate into worship. They have made gods out of one another. When this occurs, it is only a matter of time before an emotional pit will seize the soul and create this feeling of entrapment.

Bringing down and abolishing idols has to be an important step in overcoming the feeling of being trapped. This is personal work. But it is not private work!

Seventh, **learn to sacrifice praise**. What Jonah did had to be difficult. Sitting in the belly of the whale, life ebbing away, sick to death in the stench of digestive acid, Jonah began to give thanks to God. He seemingly had nothing to thank God for, so he borrowed from future blessings. He sacrificed his current feelings for a future hope. When he did this, something spiritually great happened — the feeling of being trapped fled away. Thanksgiving and "feeling trapped" cannot be housed in the same space. They won't fit together!

The life of praise is a 24-hour-a-day adventure. No matter what the outlook is, we must praise God anyway in spite of every circumstance. Praising God in the face of every circumstance will blow away every other possible negative emotion.

Lesson eight, **make your vow**. A vow is the highest form of commitment possible. You put your life on the line for a vow. A vow has to do with your life — the rest of your life.

Don't confuse making a vow to God with bargaining with God while in danger or turmoil. The difference between the two is motive.

Several times this past year I have dealt with young people on the edge of death. Every time people would pray for miracles. They would proclaim how great a testimony it would be if God healed these loved ones. The truth is, we can fool each other, but we cannot fool God. He can see ahead and knows who will be true to Him and who is just trying to use him for a healing. A vow to God is a vow of one's life unto death. The vow could involve all of one's life, or part of one's life for a specific area.

We live in a fast paced, drive-thru society that tries to avoid commitment. I actually heard a female rock star recently speak of marriage during an interview. She said she believed in matrimony, but believed that commitment should only have to last two years. I was shocked. Marriage is a life-long commitment. It is a vow. That is why we call the central part of the marital ceremony the "vows."

Vows break the feeling of being trapped because it changes our focus completely.

Finally, **when we learn the lesson; the whale will vomit us onto dry ground.** The proper attitude is, and always should be, when I finally learn the lessons God wants to teach me, he will deliver me. Jonah was delivered out of the belly of the whale.

Deliverance from feeling trapped always happens. We are either delivered from our sickness, or from our bodies. Deliverance will always occur!

### CONCLUSION

Even as I conclude this chapter, I feel a deep sense of pain for those who feel trapped. This emotional state which so many live in and go through, creates unpredictable behaviors and attitudes. Even while writing this chapter, I went through some of the things I designed, with the help of the text. If you feel trapped, you need help. These nine lessons should truly help you if you have an open mind and heart. I sincerely hope you can be open and apply these truths to your life.

Life does not have to be hell. It is only hell if you let it be. If I were using a modern adaptation, I would say, "Just say NO! (To hell, that is!).

# CHAPTER 11

## "THIS PLACE IS HELL!"

### "Purging the World"

*"But there were also false prophets among the people, just as there will be false teachers among you. They will secretly introduce destructive heresies, even denying the sovereign Lord who bought them — bringing swift destruction on themselves. Many will follow their shameful ways and will bring the way of truth into disrepute. In their greed these teachers will exploit you with stories they have made up. Their condemnation has long been hanging over them, and their destruction has not been sleeping. For if God did not spare angels when they sinned, but sent them to hell, putting them into gloomy dungeons to be held for judgment; if he did not spare the ancient world when he brought the flood on its ungodly people, but protected Noah, a preacher of righteousness, and seven others; if he condemned the cities of Sodom and Gomorrah by burning them to ashes, and made them an example of what is going to happen to the ungodly; and if he rescued Lot, a righteous man, who was distressed by the filthy lives of lawless men (for that righteous man, living among them day after day, was tormented in his righteous soul by the lawless deeds he saw and heard) — if this is so, then the Lord knows how to rescue godly men from trials and to hold the unrighteous for the day of judgment, while continuing their punishment. This is especially true of those who follow the corrupt desire of the sinful nature and despise authority. Bold and arrogant, these men are not afraid to slander celestial beings; yet even angels, although they are stronger and more powerful, do not*

*bring slanderous accusations against such beings in the presence of the Lord. But these men blaspheme in matters they do not understand. They are like brute beasts, creatures of instinct, born only to be caught and destroyed, and like beasts they too will perish."* — *2 Peter 2:1-12*

Q: Why is there such a thing as hell?

A: To purge the world of all evil. This answer comes after much in-depth study on the place called hell. No matter how in depth the study, <u>purging</u> is God's intention.

In the new heaven and new earth, as recorded in Revelation 21, there will be no evil. It will be gone, but not without a fight! Evil will take many with it. Those left will be righteous of heart.

II Peter 2:1-12 should be examined to give direction in this matter.

## BE DISCERNING, NOT DECEIVED  v. 1-4

"Satan is like a roaring lion seeking whom he will devour." Satan <u>hates</u> the Christian! Although Satan does not have the power God does, he knows our weaknesses. That is exactly where he is going to hit us.

Where is your weakness? Do you find yourself gravitating towards preaching or teaching that condones your vice? It really is natural to do. I list my beliefs, then I find a church that believes the way I do.

We have to be open! God is not finished with us at all. Our only concern should be "Is the Bible being preached?" When discerning a teaching, ask three questions:

1. Is it based on Biblical truths?

2. Is it consistent with what I know about God?

3. Would Jesus believe it?

**Is it based on Biblical truths?** Dig! Find out! <u>Everything</u> we do must be based on a Biblical truth! If it is just based on psychology, don't make it part of your life. If it is just physical, don't allow it to be part of your life. Yes, the life is three parts, body, mind and spirit. But understand the Bible is the governor for all three!

**Is it consistent with what I know about God?** God's Holy Spirit <u>does</u> reveal himself to us. He directs us. He is with us. How does this teaching set with you? Ask," How do I feel about it on the inside?"

**Would Jesus Christ advocate it?** This is an all-encompassing question. What would Jesus do?

Even after asking these three questions, the way can still be deceptive. There is really no big sign a false teacher wears about his neck saying: "I am a false teacher." They all will have a different look or approach, but notice, *"Who privily shall bring in damnable heresies."* "Privily" means clever. Many people are clever. Someone who is "cleverly bringing" knows in their heart they are bringing heresy.

There are many faith healers that plant people in audiences to "increase people's faith." *"For it is by faith you are made whole."* They problem is: The faith that effects change is a spiritual faith that comes as a result of God's indwelling Holy Spirit. It is not the emotion of a moment, but an eternity of God's destiny. The type of faith that heals, is one of eyes set on God so fixed, that a healing has already come — a healing of one's faith in God. When my eyes are fixed on God, who cares how and when He will heal? It doesn't matter if the healing is now or in glory, *"For to me to live is Christ, but for me to die is gain."*

If a teaching is not to be found in the Bible, what foundation does it have? Verse two gives us a foundation for discerning false teaching: "if the way of truth is spoken evil of,"or if Christ is denied. Without Christ there is no salvation.

False teaching also gives tolerance to the sex sin, or advocates physical fulfillment outside of holy matrimony. False teaching tells you what is pleasant to your body, not what is good for your soul.

False teachers are brought to swift destruction (verse one). God did not spare the angels that sinned. He will not tolerate these false teachers, either.

Hell and destruction are where evil like this belongs. God uses hell to <u>purge</u> the world of evil. He uses false teachers to pull out the ones who are not grounded, to separate the righteous from the unrighteous. It separates the sheep from the goats. Think of it: The strong become stronger.

## THE LORD DELIVERS THE GODLY v. 5-9

Deliverance was based upon their spiritual condition, the righteousness of their hearts. God knows what truly motivates us, even when those closest to us have doubts.

Peter uses examples of Noah who built the ark amidst a perverse generation. God did not single Noah out just because he liked the way he parted his hair, but because God knew Noah's heart.

Lot was spared the fate of Sodom and Gomorrah even amidst their perversion. Verse eight says that Lot was vexed. We can become vexed at work among the heathen, but we can still remain righteous. We will not succumb to temptation if our heart is right.

Of course, living in the advent of the New Testament, righteousness of God means accepting Christ as Savior. Once we have done that, we become "right" before God. Thus begins a relationship with God in a personal way.

When temptation happens, God makes deliverance available. The choice of giving in depends upon each person. The "deck" is never stacked completely against us. Yet, God will not force us to go against our own will. If we have committed our life to Christ, however, our will should be God's will.

A person may feel dirty by being around filth, but inside he/she can be perfectly clean. God is so good to us, especially when we are in a jam. He is so merciful, even when we are living in a corrupt and vile age. He knows my heart and is good to me. He will deliver me from temptation because he knows within my heart I don't want to give in.

## CUT PEOPLE SLACK  v. 10-11

Jesus talked about picking splinters out of others' eyes when we have boards in our own. We all have different pressures and pains, problems and trials.

Each of us has different responsibilities and personalities. Different things "trip our triggers." In areas of interest, we all vary. It seems, however, that we sometimes expect everyone to behave like we do and fully understand us. One of the most important things we can do in our society today is to **cut people slack**. The key is this: Be considerate without compromising. Even though someone really did us wrong, let's make excuses for him or her. The world would be a much better place. In fact, we might even begin to believe it ourselves.

If your personality is like mine, this is hard to do. The basic step is to make excuses for others. The second step is to exhibit a gentle spirit. Become "easier" on people. The third step is to ask yourself, How would Jesus react to this?

Not even the angels in heaven rally accusations against the lustful person, or the one with self-will, or even the busy body. The angels are more powerful and mightier than man is, but they will not accuse.

## BE OPEN TO GOD'S VOICE!

The problem the false teachers had was they were closed. They had all the answers. They did whatever felt good. The good feeling physically is often the worst thing you can do to yourself.

False teachers laugh at things they don't know about. Often the things that are considered "sissy" are just what they need. They just haven't tried it and don't know anything about it. Their destiny is set. They are no better than the demon powers that will burn forever. In God's purging of the world of evil, God is no respecter of persons. Yet God is not willing that any should perish.

# CHAPTER 12

# "GOING THROUGH HELL!"

*"Therefore the grave enlarges its appetite and opens its mouth without limit; into it will descend their nobles and masses with all their brawlers and revelers."*
— *Isaiah 5:14*

It is important to include a chapter on this if we are going to take a comprehensive look at hell. Hell is a definite place or dimension. That truth should be of primary importance to us. We have already looked at several different areas on the topic of hell. "Where", "Why"" and "What for?" are types of questions that always help to broaden us. One of the major purposes of this study is to realize hell is a very positive thing. **Yes, I said it is a positive thing!**

Not only is hell a place or dimension as has been commonly thought. There are also times that develop when we feel like we are going through hell.

In chapter ten, we looked at life as hell in the sense of being trapped. Now we are going to look at going through hell in this life. Please understand that this is in no way meant to develop a new doctrine or religion. This is spiritually not deep, but it is life. There are times when hell simply seems to be at hand. Jesus taught often of the Kingdom of Heaven being at hand. He was directing us inward. The Kingdom of Heaven that was at hand, as he indicated further is "within you."

Although the phrase "going through hell" is not something I let my kids say, it is a place where many seem to be. They feel like they are going through hell in their lives. Let me say that I believe hell is a place far, far worse than anything that could happen in this life, even multiplied 100 fold. Hell will be so ugly and so eternal, that we cannot even attempt to know the depth of the pain. Even so, we should look at some areas in the human endeavor, which seem to us like we are going through hell.

My areas of choice do not exhaust this subject. I don't know how I could ever develop a comprehensive list. Over the several days as I was writing this material, my list grew and grew. Even so, these areas will seem to have many of the same resolves to them. In some instances the only answer is to brace up and be strong! Above all, let us be as patient and as understanding of people at all times, as is absolutely possible. May we realize that even the worst of all temporal suffering is much better than a literal hell. May we use those times when it seems we are going through hell, to prompt our resolve to never experience the eternal hell. May it be so!

## THE LOSS OF SOMEONE YOU LOVE

Losing a loved one is right at the top of the list of the most stressful times in one's life. It takes a long time to work through the loss of a loved one. The intensity with which grief affects you is based upon how close you were to the one you lost. In the bottom line analysis, the hardest emotional issue to deal with is the finality of the event. Realizing that you will never see this person again in this life is often emotionally insurmountable.

In my booklet, "Handling Death, Dying, and Grief, I dealt with this very important issue of grief cycles. Grief comes in waves. For a while it seems you are doing okay and then, "Wham-o!" you are overcome by emotion. You may or may not know what triggered it. Go ahead and forge on through these cycles. Cry, weep, wail and moan. Talk and work it out. Don't feel bad or embarrassed. This is grief therapy.

The reason it seems like hell is when the ability to grieve is suppressed. You may feel embarrassed, or think it is a sign of weakness. When this happens, life becomes practically unbearable. We must be allowed to grieve.

The sting of a loss is around for a long, long time. It is present and active for years. Yet through the times of grief, one very precious element comes to the surface that makes life bearable — memory. The memories you have with a loved one is what will help take you through the rest of your life. Creating memories requires the commitment of people who want to gain all there is in life to have. Building memories requires the dedication of people to put others first. Don't worry about the money. It is here today and gone tomorrow. Memories last forever.

If you didn't learn this lesson until it was too late, maybe you feel guilty and bad memories are the only ones you have of a loved one. Then release yourself from this private hell by centering in on one or two or three good, decent memories of the loved one you are grieving over. Center in on these, and allow them to be what you think of when you think of that person. Release yourself from the torment and bondage of your mind!

## DIVORCE

Many say divorce is much like death. I can see why they say it, but I have always thought divorce was worse than death emotionally.

The emotional part of a divorce runs a gamut of all possible feelings. Divorce has touched us all in some way personally. No one who has had to deal with divorce personally wonders why God hates it so. We all hate what it does. It is like "going through hell" as most would testify. Divorce happens to people. It has to be dealt with as it comes.

Divorce affects every area of a life. It touches the extended family. Rarely do people who are contemplating a divorce realize just how far it extends. Often we assume that once the parties involved find out how far the divorce emotionally extends, they would back out. But generally, by the time this realization occurs, too much "water has gone under the bridge."

The part of the divorce that makes life seem like hell is all of the hurt. Just the idea of ripping a shared relationship completely apart brings some hurt. Add to this all the things which are said, secrets revealed, and true feelings coming out, and soon resentment and bitterness evolve from these hurt feelings. The things that are said can cripple self-esteem (which we will address later).

There are many ways to deal with emotional hurt. The first thing is to try your best not to see another person as the subject of your problem, nor the reason for your hurt. If you allow yourself time to become bitter toward someone else, you end up taking animosity out upon others. Your own loved ones who are trying to show you love and support generally bear the brunt of your animosity. This must be avoided.

By internalizing your hurt, you will ask yourself the question, "Why do I hurt?" You can then gain new insight into yourself. Hurtful circumstances can actually become purgers of one's own defective personality traits. Internalize.

The second help in dealing with emotional hurt is to stay busy and keep your mind occupied. During key times, one can never be too busy. Many would disagree with this theory, but the truth is, a divorce creates too many aspects to deal with at one time. The mind cannot emotionally handle all of it at once. The things you deal with which are hurtful should only be let in a little at a time.

The third help in dealing with emotional hurt is to constantly remind yourself how important you are to God. Think of the price Jesus paid for your spiritual redemption. Constantly remind yourself that no matter how desolate you feel emotionally, spiritually everything is fine. Don't allow yourself to feel that your spiritual barometer and emotional barometer are the same. They are different. Remind yourself of God's love and you won't even feel like hell!

## ADDICTION

Addiction is the psychological or physical dependency on something. There are many, many different kinds of addictions. An addict is an addict because of an addictive personality. People with addictive personalities are the ones you would want to have undertake a project, because they will go all out and all the way. They get things done. The problem is, they can destroy their lives the same way!

An addiction creates its own kind of hell. Alcoholic's Anonymous has created one of many recovery programs for addicts. In their program, they have implemented what is called the Twelve-Step Plan. If properly applied and carefully executed, this Twelve-Step Plan provides the addict with a behavioral model.

Whatever the addiction, one must realize they are unable to overcome the problem on their own. Then they must look to God to empower them. Next the addict must create boundaries to build a model for behavior. It is also important to create a group of people to be accountable to, to help develop a channel of responsibility. This is not an attempt to rewrite or redefine the Twelve Step Recovery program, but to emphasize some important components of recovery for the addict.

Most importantly, an addict needs to turn his or her life completely over to the Lord Jesus Christ. The most important way to overcome an addiction is to become a disciple of Jesus and a follower of His Word. Without these essential ingredients the addict is virtually doomed.

There are many good recovery programs. In my ministry I have been involved extensively with many different kinds of addicts. From alcoholics, to cocaine, to sex, to work — there are many different kinds of addicts. The only programs that really work for people are those which make Jesus Christ the "higher power." Even then the addict requires constant maintenance and help – sometimes even on an hour-to-hour basis.

There is hope for any addict. It does not have to be the private hell it puts the addict and his loved ones through!

## SELF-ESTEEM

Self-esteem problems have many different origins. They are primarily based upon inadequacies in upbringing or in dysfunctional conditioning. Either way, a low sense of self-esteem has to do with conditioning. Some of the problems related to self-esteem are things like insecurity, fear, defensiveness and a lack of confidence, relationship problems, personality conflicts, the need for attention, and many other possible problems as well.

Self esteem problems can create great mental torture and torment. People with these kinds of problems really do feel like they are going through hell.

There is healing for self-esteem. The healing that is required takes time and is a long, slow process. The conditioning that created low self-esteem must be replaced by a relationship with Jesus Christ. This relationship cannot afford to be status quo. It must be a growing, dynamic relationship that constantly demands one to yield every area of one's life to him.

# PAIN

Thirty minutes ago I was with an older lady who had just undergone a surgery to remove some pins in her leg. She had carried these pins for six months. She broke her leg from a fall. She is 93 years old and has been in constant pain from it. Last night her headache was so bad she did not get any sleep. They say her headache was a result of all the drugs she took because of the surgery. She was in excruciating pain, and exhausted from a lack of sleep. I felt terrible for her. Prayer seemed like such a little thing to do facing such enormous pain. It is a hard thing to admit but so many times prayer seems like such a small thing to do for people who are in such pain.

Not long ago a man in my congregation had bone cancer. Over the next eighteen months I watched him die. The physical pain he endured caused him to lose his mind. Day after day, hour after hour, minute after minute, the pain went on and on. They gave him every kind of possible drug to gain some relief. They gave him steroids. Finally they surgically removed his nerve endings to give him some relief. They sent him home from the hospital with two weeks to live. He lasted three months. I prayed with him often. He would come and go out of his coma. His faith in my prayers were greater then my prayers. Often I would wonder how could my prayers help his pain, but they always seemed to. It was something miraculous. It was God's grace. Day after day I would look into his eyes, his body and mind twisted by the pain that tormented him night and day.

Through this three-month experience I began to see the pain of hell. I know it was not even close to the pain of eternal torment but I sensed the immensity of and depth of the pain in the physical part of life. Bob had faith in God and in my prayers. He is no longer in pain. Bob is in heaven. At his funeral I shared these thoughts with the people who had gathered. A great peace swept over me as I shared the honest truth of my feelings during the closing days of his life. In the room he died, there was peace. We all knew that his death was for the best. He suffered enormously. No one who experienced those hours could have ever had pat answers for this human experience.

Pain management is something hospitals have been getting into in recent years. Through counseling, behavioral approaches, and electronic therapy many people have been helped. Pain is miserable. It can actually drive people crazy if it is not managed.

I knew a man who had a stroke. He was paralyzed on his left side. It affected his speech. He could not even say his name. A couple of times per week he had seizures. His wife called these little strokes. I was there many times when he had these strokes. He underwent indescribable pain. The screams of pain came from his soul. It was thoroughly unbelievable. I will never forget how even in his worst moments I would pray and the pain would cease. He could never communicate with me but he understood what I asked God for. After a prayer he would be pain free for several hours.

I have many stories of people who have endured the "pain of hell." More than the pain we must develop some points of deliverance for people in pain. These points must be applied now to make them a part of your life before the pain comes. To put these points off is to put your deliverance off. These points of deliverance are an investment in your life before your pain begins. They must be learned now!

**Prayer helps relieve pain!**

It helps. God wants to relieve you of some of your pain. He will relieve you of the intensity of your pain in direct proportion to your faith's ability to help you. This has nothing to do with who prays, but who is in pain. If you believe God wants to help you he will help you. The edge of your pain will subside. There is actually a metaphysical phenomenon in this application. Pain impulses come through the brain. The brain is the message center. The brain regulates the body chemistry. This body chemistry changes the bodily functions. If you believe in something strong enough, it will alter your body chemistry. When the composition alters, so does the pain level.

## Develop new thought processes!

Thinking can improve your level of pain if you work to harness it. There is tremendous power in thinking to harness pain. The more you divert your mental attention away from your pain, from the source of your pain, the greater the possibilities of relief become. Divert your attention away from the pain source and you will harness the pain area.

## Modern technology!

Many people with back pain are now using various techniques of modern technology to relieve their pain. Electrical impulses sent to nerve endings is now one of the very basic techniques. These new techniques should not be overlooked. All three of these should be applied equally.

## ANGER

Many fields of psychology have spent years-studying anger. Our understanding of anger has developed considerably over recent years. Expressions of anger vary greatly. It can be from the violence of a mass murderer on one hand to a stutterer on the other end. The reasons for anger vary as well — things like a dominating mother to child molestation held secret for years. Things like a lack of attention or a divorce can produce a lifelong problem of deep-seated anger. A reason why anger is such a problem to study is because it is hard to cross-index it. Anger can only be studied person to person and case by case. Different things bring out different reactions from people.

With all this in mind, anger holds its victim a prisoner. This is why it is included in the "going through hell" section. It is totally unpredictable. It surfaces at unpredictable times and in unpredictable intensities. Anger usually does permanent damage. The emotion that causes damage is usually identified as anger.

Anger is such a deep-seated emotion that its victims are not able to receive real help because of a lack of openness. It really is not the victim's fault because it requires some head on, highly confrontational intervention to help a person with deep-seated problems with anger. There are a couple of ways to help a person going through this kind of personal "hell."


## Confront openly but give them their space.

An angry person will act like there is no problem. They will seem to know all of the answers. Inside they want you to confront them, but externally they want to act like there is no problem. Confront them with what you know about their behavior. Make sure you reinforce your care for them. Brace yourself for their response. They will exhibit a lot of anger because they are being confronted. It will take some time, but it will sink in on them.


## Get in the trenches to help.

Don't hold back. Help them. Each of us must win the right to be heard. Our society sees people as disposable. It is a thing in our culture. We must be careful not to see one another this way. We need to see people as priceless treasures with unlimited potential. Each person is well worth any risk. We must help people be released from this bondage!

## EMPLOYMENT DIFFICULTIES

Many people have trouble at work. Whether it is problems with the employer, employee or coworkers. Very few of us are not affected by work-related problems. Because we have to face these problems on a day-to-day basis, it is as if many of us have to "go through hell" constantly.

These work-related troubles are extremely subjective to each person's feelings. There are so many dynamics in the workplace that one certain model or suggestion is difficult to develop since there are so many different variables. There are three things that should be applied to every work place. The first thing is **love.** Love is a very special spiritual healer. It is required of every Christian believer. The second thing is **patience.** We must be patient with others. Patiently enduring creates great inward strength. The third thing is **understanding.** Try to put yourself in the shoes of another. Ask God to give you empathy toward, and for, others.

If you are going through a work problem right now, you may not be open to these three elements. They may sound too simple or you may take issue with them. If the truth is known, the problem with these three elements is a lack of initiative to try them. They must be properly executed. They must be executed consistently. Most people are too lazy to work through work problems. We want the easy way out. In the face of conflict we need to brace up and work through our employment difficulties.

# FINANCIAL SETBACKS

Financial pressures can absolutely devastate a person's life personally and professionally. Whether it is just a cash flow problem, a setback, a loss of income or job, or total bankruptcy, financial problems can last a short or a long time. The distress it causes can seem like one is going through hell.

Finances are the biggest source of conflict in homes. It creates tension, conflict and confusion. There are some appropriate behaviors in our financial lives that we need to develop.

Everyone needs personal guidelines for one's finances. They need to be personal and tailor made to you. Once developed, they need to be applied. Only you can apply your personal guidelines.

Next, your guidelines must be implemented consistently. The truth is, it does not matter what your plan is as long as you apply it consistently. Any financial plan adhered to consistently will bail you out of any hole you have gotten yourself into.

Digging yourself out of your financial hole requires a commitment to learn from your lessons of the past. Repeating the same pattern is a surprising error many make. Many people make the same mistake over and over and over again. We must learn from our mistakes and develop new patterns.

# LONELINESS

Loneliness affects the lives of millions of people. They come from all walks of life. They live alone as well as in homes with many people. Loneliness is a state of mind, not a station in life.

Loneliness is a result of people centering in upon themselves. They allow themselves the option of keeping their feelings in and keeping to themselves. Many times loneliness begins out of a person's insecurity of being around people.

The key to battling loneliness is to open up and take chances. Don't be afraid of people. Take some risks. You won't get along with everyone, but you will get along with some. Don't live in the fear of being rejected. The "hell" in loneliness is simply not worth it.

## DOMESTIC DIFFICULTIES

There are so many different potential domestic difficulties in our society. Things like child abuse or child molestation leave families with deep scars. Even with intense therapy, these problems are ones which families can carry with them for years. Many go through their own kind of "hell" enduring it.

Every family needs to resolve to treat one another as a priceless treasure. We need to allow one another space to develop opportunities to grow. We should express love freely and communicate honestly. Openness between family members should be the rule and not the exception.

The list goes on and on. Many of the areas we discussed can be transferred to other areas. These models should be transferred and applied. Each of us needs to help others along the way to help, encourage, and guide. Many people just lose their direction out of frustration and burden. With simple commitment and consistency we can overcome this kind of hell!

# CHAPTER 13

## "THE LOOK OF HELL"

She was the church-paid baby-sitter and he was on the pastoral staff. She would come to the church to get the nursery ready for Sunday. His office was right next door. She started by sticking her head in to say hello. Eventually her visits got longer. Then they became intimate. Somewhere, they crossed the line and became adulterers.

Where is the line? How is it that people cross over it? Do people realize that a moment or two of physical pleasure may result in years of needed therapy?

This chapter is not about the slow degenerative process of sin nor is it about the heat of the moment. It is about drawing lines and defining boundaries in our personal lives — even in our deeply personal lives. These areas of life vary greatly from person to person. What is the point of departure? When is the point crossed and hell takes over? These are questions each of us must answer for ourselves. Combating the look of hell, we must develop lifelong principles to guide us.

> *"Death and Destruction are never satisfied, and neither are the eyes of man."* — *Proverbs 27:20*

Call it what you will, but we must acknowledge human frailties. This acknowledgment should not be a cop out, but rather a warning signal.

Several months ago the amber-colored emissions light came on in the dash of my car. I have always been sensitive about warning lights. I was frantic. Before I tore off to the garage I decided to read the owner's manual. The way I understand it, this light was programmed to come on at around 60,000 miles by a microchip. When it comes on, you are supposed to take your vehicle into the factory garage to have everything checked out. I don't want to offend those who work on cars. Nevertheless, I want to say I think the American public is getting ripped off. This maintenance light was intended to look like a warning light to alarm the owner. The owner generally panics and takes the vehicle into the garage. The next thing you know, there are many things which need to be done to your car. Any car on the road could "need" to have $2,000 worth of work done on it easily.

This same problem occurs in our spiritual lives. Sure we know we are frail, but we ignore the warning signs of trouble. We ignore the warning signs because we really don't know who we can trust. When we begin to ignore things that could warn of impending destruction we develop a "loser" form of living. The bottom line is: **Don't ignore true warning signs of problems in your lifestyle.**

Satisfaction as a word is a wonderful experience. Yet, satisfaction is a downright hard thing to find. A lack of satisfaction is really a part of our original sin. The way it becomes manifest is in the sense of the more people get, the more they seem to want. Nothing ever satisfies them. They are never at peace. They are never settled down. I am one of these people. It is hard for me to admit this. My church is never big enough.... People never work hard enough.... I never make enough money... on and on. I am rarely settled or satisfied. It is a spiritual problem and I want to overcome it.

The scary thing about my problem is how Scripture addresses it. The scenario I draw between my desires and the destruction of hell prompts me to want to work on this problem and get it behind me. It is not something that can be overcome in an hour or two. It starts with a resolve. The resolve is to start working toward the solution.

Maybe you have the same problem I do. Maybe it is a lack of satisfaction in a specific area like your spouse, children, marriage, job, or finances. It could be you have prayed and prayed about your lack of contentment, but to no avail. I believe the only way to deal with it is to see it as a spiritual problem. There is a line we cross which has allowed a discontentment to develop. Let's draw the line again. Crossing it will sound off an alarm. Our line should be this way: **I will be satisfied every day, moment by moment, as I live by faith, obedient to Jesus.**

No matter what life has to bring, I am determined to be satisfied. Being in the center of God's will brings satisfaction enough.

There are other ways to keep ourselves from small temptations that tend to create an atmosphere where we feel comfortable to step over the line we draw. Temptations are the "hook" of hell. These little things occur to keep us away from the course we know we are to stay on. Undergoing a temptation is not sin. Succumbing to a temptation is sin.

> *"A man who strays from the path of understanding comes to rest in the company of the dead."* — *Proverbs 21:16*

For many years I have said that Satan cannot read your thoughts, but he can supplant thoughts into your brain. Satan only knows if he has gotten through if we yield to a temptation. This is why Scripture challenges us to be sober and vigilant when dealing with Satan who wants to devour us. There comes a point of devouring. It occurs when we depart from the principles we know to be true. It may be a simple point to make in light of such a powerful Scripture but devastation comes by crossing over the line. We need to draw yet another line: **Stay true to what you know to be true!**

Don't give in one inch from the truth. Don't depart from the rights and wrongs in your life. Most importantly, don't allow the passion of the moment to expose yourself to losing everything. The Old Testament story of Jacob and Esau is so relevant to our modern world. Jacob was the Mama's boy making the evening meal. Esau was the oldest twin and his father's favorite. Esau was hairy, rugged and a great outdoorsman. Everything his father Isaac owned would go to the firstborn son. Esau was the heir.

One day while he was hunting, Esau became famished. When he got home he found Jacob making soup. When he asked his brother for some, Jacob took full advantage of the situation. Jacob offered him some soup for the full right of birth of his firstborn position. Esau was very hungry. He traded his birth right for some soup. Jacob became the firstborn son on that day. Esau traded something eternal for something temporal.

Most everything in life requires some kind of trade off. The reason we fall into hell and destruction is because we cross over the lines we draw. We trade something eternal for something temporal.

The whole idea of eternal torment is enough motivation for many people to mend their ways and change their life. Every time we are faced with temporal pleasure we must discipline our minds to center in and focus on eternal goals.

Whether it is immoral sexual pleasure or an impure thought, they are all selfish acts. Selfish acts are temporal pleasures. They can actually put our eternal destinies in question. Many people believe once a person is saved they can never lose their salvation. They believe that you can trade something eternal for something temporal and still make it to heaven. In another chapter we will study the "citizens of hell." These are people who trade their eternal destiny for a temporal pleasure. They must realize how vital it is to come to grips with what they are doing. The lines we draw must keep this in mind all the time.

*"The path of life leads upward for the wise to keep him from going down to the grave."* — Proverbs 15:24

The lines we draw for personal conduct are very individual. What one person can do, another may not be able to. From time to time we all adjust our lines to accommodate more activity. This procedure can be a hook from hell all of its own. The path that leads to eternal life draws its lines in; it does not let them out!

This can be a great test to see where you are spiritually and to see if hell is about to hook you: Are your lines of behavior bold and definite? Do you know where you stand on various lifestyle issues?

Where you draw your lines is a very important concept. Don't let yourself off easy. Remember: Decisions are made before the passion of the moment.

Everyone must draw bold lines, never to cross over. Many non-Christians I have talked to believe they are in full control of everything. They deceive themselves. All of us can be enticed. Enticement is a trick of the devil. It is the heartbeat of hell.

**Enticement appears sweet and smooth but it is really destructive and deadly.** In the book of Proverbs sweet and smooth are qualities of the "strange woman." These can be qualities of anything appealing — even anything enticing. It would teach us all to not allow ourselves the chance of being enticed by watching our emotions. Be careful. Her end will kill. Before killing, it causes a slow painful death. Her feet go down to death. We must keep our eyes open all the time. Enticement blinds us all!

As hard as we try, we are not able to second-guess enticement. We always have the chance of being enticed as long as we breathe. God wants us to realize that we are vulnerable. That way we can become completely dependent upon him. If we think we have enticement all figured out, we won't depend upon Jesus like we should. "In all thy ways acknowledge him."

Proverbs 7:26 goes further to graphically illustrate this point:

*"For she hath cast down many wounded: yea many strong men have been slain by her."*

We need to learn from the mistakes of these strong men. Every day our prayer should be: "Lord, I lean on you, help me to keep my eyes open and upon you at all times." Enticement is real. Don't be enticed — don't turn your eyes away!

Proverbs 9:17 says *"stolen waters are sweet, and bread eaten in secret is pleasant."* Succumbing to enticement may bring temporary pleasure but the next verse goes on to say that her guests are in the depths: *"knoweth not that the dead are there."* So many people need to be shaken up. So many people have been enticed. It looks so good. If feels so good. It is so deadly. Don't be enticed — be careful!

**The only way of avoidance is staying clear.** Proverbs 5:7-11 tells us to remove thy way far from her. Don't even go close to her. No matter what the reason. The first thing each of us must do is **identify our weaknesses.** Once identified, each of us has a better grip on what to avoid. We all have weak areas. Those who think they are spiritual supermen will wind up in hell.

"Don't even go to the door." Don't be afraid to run. Use holy feet! Turn your tails and run. Run for your life — your spiritual life. God has a wonderful plan for each of us. According to verse 9 all those good things will be passed on to others if we turn from Him. Further, not only will we spend eternity in hell, generally life will be hell-like as well. The pain that will consume us will far outweigh the pleasure gained.

**Avoid regret.** Proverbs 5:12-13 says that hell is a place for eternal regret. If we heed the warnings we can avoid the regrets.

Look at the enticement episode in Genesis 3:1-7:

**Why did she eat?**

> ➢ **She saw the tree was good.** The serpent enticed her to believe the pleasure gained would far outweigh the surrounding circumstances.

> ➢ **It was pleasant to the eye.** It was pleasant to the eye of the one who had not prayed about it first. Prayer will reveal the truth. We have to wait in the attitude of prayer.

> ➢ **She desired to be like God.** She didn't recognize her own weaknesses. She didn't run for her life; instead, she took some fruit to Adam.

We need to know our weaknesses and avoid them. Avoid enticement by drawing your lines. Most importantly, **reevaluate your lines occasionally.**

So many examples could be given of people who have fallen into the devil's trap. It seems like we are his personal projects. He follows us, tempts us, and tries to influence us. The truth is Satan can only know us if we succumb to his temptations. It simply does not have to happen.

> *"The dead are in deep anguish, those beneath the waters and all that live in them."*  — Job 26:5

This is a graphic description of hell. The word "waters" is the Hebrew word (mayim) which means urine or excrete. Hell as it is used here is for those people who did not draw their lines. They pressed the borders. They enlarged their boundaries. They drifted off into the gray areas. Don't end up in this eternal torment. Brace up. Draw your lines.

# CHAPTER 14

## "THE CITIZENS OF HELL"

Hollywood has been depicting hell on the screen for years. Many jokes have been told. Many yarns have been spun. Many late-night stories have been told of the sights and sounds of hell. No other Scripture gives us such a graphic description as Revelation 21:8 of the citizens of hell:

> *"But the cowardly, the unbelieving, the vile, the murderers, the sexually immoral, those who practice magic arts, the idolaters and all liars — their place will be in the fiery lake of burning sulfur. This is the second death."* — Revelation 21:8

> *"Their part in the lake which burns with fire and brimstone..."*

This gives us the composition of the lake of fire. The lake of fire is the essence of ugliness, evil, and the purging of evil. It will be here that all things evil will be forever and ever.

We have already looked at why this has to occur. God desires to purge the universe of evil. The whole idea of a lake "burning" is this concept. The Greek word for burning is Kaio and means to consume. Fire will totally envelop and hold prisoner the entire realm of evil.

"Brimstone" is a word I have heard used in many contexts. It is greatly misunderstood. It once was used in describing preaching styles. In the olden days, "hellfire and brimstone" preaching was a positive remark. Now, it is thought of as uneducated, unsophisticated, and unintellectual.

"Brimstone" is really not a preaching style at all. It comes from the ancient word "theion" which has as its basis "theos" or God concept. It seems that brimstone is properly interpreted — God like illumination. In its application, we see that those who spend eternity in the lake of fire will have the knowledge of God continually in their existence.

We could go many directions with this application of brimstone. One thing that might occur is that those in the lake of fire will be able to look out and see the glory of heaven. This is a similar picture to Lazarus and the rich man. Another thing we could apply is the fact that these souls will be in an existent state. They will not perish or soul sleep. (Many world religions teach this aspect of eternity.) These souls damned because of their lack of faith in Christ Jesus will be in an eternal tormented state of existence.

Another thing we need to consider is that the lake of fire is created and energized by God. God has created this place for the entire dimension of evil. This will be its composition. God will organize it completely. Many people are under the impression that the lake of fire will be run by the chief source of evil, Satan. The truth is, Satan will only be a citizen of hell. The lake of fire will be intensely gruesome torment. There will be no reason for Satan to organize it.

The Scripture in Revelation 21:8 cites that these things listed shall have their part in the lake of fire. This list is the composition of the lake. These are the citizens of hell. This is hell. We have a tendency to forget that without people, there is no town. The size of the town is based upon the amount of people. Although God knows how big the lake of fire will be, He is not making that predetermination for us. The lake of fire will be as big or as small as it needs to be.

Let's make the lake of fire as little as possible! Since the time of Jesus, He has been at the right hand of the Father. He left us in charge of reaching the lost. He made us responsible for reaching people. The fewer people there, the smaller it will be.

Finally, I think all those in heaven will always be conscious of the existence of the lake of fire. It will somehow be a part of the landscape. It may appear as the sun or a moon, or a star off in the distance. I think we will always sense its presence.

The work God is doing in our world has eternal dimensions. We should never take anything lightly. Heaven and hell are just one heartbeat away for any of us. Every day of our lives is important in the sense of our eternal destiny. What we do or don't do will affect us forever and might affect others forever as well.

The Scripture in Revelation 21:8 does something quite amazing by listing the citizens of hell by categories. Is this a complete list? There was certainly nothing limiting God when giving the list. Through careful examination we are able to see that the things on the list are fairly complete. Most of them are self-explanatory. There have been many explanations of these eight things. Some have said they were behaviors to avoid. Some have said that if you do these things, you will fall from grace. Still others have said you can never fall from grace, but these eight behaviors are a symbol that shows whether you are really saved or not.

All of this discussion is unnecessary. These eight spirits named want desperately to possess the soul. If you allow them in, they will take you to the lake of fire. I have never thought God desired to send anyone to hell. If you allow these in your life, they will take you there. Use this information to test yourself and your life. Each of us might sense a trace of these in our lives — let the Holy Spirit convict you and strengthen you. Start over again.

## FEARFULNESS

The first group of people to be mentioned is the fearful. The thought of fearfulness conjures up the notion of little children scared of the dark. Fearfulness is really more defined than what we have always thought. There are several spirits of fear. These spirits can all rob people of their quality of life.

**The first spirit of fear is the worrywart.** This person worries about everything. They can drive themselves and those around them crazy with their worrisome spirit. This person simply cannot seem to turn over every bit of their lives to Jesus. The worrywart is really not saved because Jesus takes away the anxieties of life! With that said, are there traces of the worrisome spirit in your life? Purge your life of these areas before the lake of fire has to. Worrisome attitudes have no place in the kingdom of God or in the life of the Christian believer.

**The second spirit of fear is the terror of God.** The fear of God has always meant the reverence of God. We have taken this phrase to an extreme. God loves us and, through Jesus, desires to have a personal relationship with us. We don't have to be terrorized by God. The sense of being terrorized by God comes from our own sense of guilt in our lives. We sense the guilt of our behavior and deep down we know we will pay for our sins. The person who is terrorized by God usually generates an image that he has everything under control and knows where he stands with God. These people desperately need the Lord. They very much want to be relieved of their "ugly God" mentality. They need to be introduced to and shown a different kind of Jesus than they have previously known.

**The third spirit of fear is the faithless.** These people don't believe in God's power to change the course of world events. This disbelief is often guarded and never revealed. They are afraid of the news. They are afraid for their health. They are paranoid about their bodies. They think everything is cancer. They sleep with guns in their beds. They need balance in their lives. They need to learn that faith is doing your best and turning it all over to God. This is the essence of faith. This is the faith that brings one joy in life. Without it they are fearful and miserable.

**The final spirit of fear is timidity.** The place timidity shows out the most is in prayer life. Do you ask God for great things? Do you expect great things from God? Christians often forget the great power in prayer through the Holy Spirit. Being timid not only keeps us from having all the good things God wants us to have, it also limits our faith. When we are timid, the faith we have shrinks up.

## UNBELIEVING

The original Greek word is "apistos," which means "without Christian faith." The people who will burn forever and ever in the lake of fire will be those who have not made the Christian faith their system of worship. This is not some Bible thumping fundamentalist yelling from a street corner. It is not some sectarian approach. It is simply the truth.

I have always resented the street preacher. The street preachers in our town shout dogmatically at all the cars traveling by. They yell and shout that we are all going to hell. They are part of a Bible college that requires them to do this type of "ministry" one day per week as part of their course of study. It always bothers me how they could yell and scream at people they don't even know. Yet, I see their aggressiveness comes from their conviction to convert as many non-believers as possible.

I don't really want to get off on Methodism. What is most important is that we fully realize that the only ones who will inherit eternal life are those who follow Jesus Christ. The English Bible as we know it does not make Christ a prophet, but the Son of God. Just today I got involved in a rather lengthy discussion with someone regarding this very issue.

To believe in Jesus, as the Son of God is not an option to get to heaven, it is by Jesus' own testimony the only way to get there. Believing in Jesus is not just a head thing — it has to be a life thing. Believing in Jesus means to follow Him by first denying oneself.

Conceptualizing Jesus Christ as the Son of God requires us to believe in both His virgin birth and His resurrection from the dead. The person I was discussing this whole issue with remarked that their church never got hung up on the virgin birth. I made it clear to him then, and us now, that it is a critical issue. We either profess it or deny it. Jesus is either the Son of God or a prophet. There is no middle of the road regarding this issue. The choice is up to each of us.

Many people wonder about those who have never heard of Jesus such as Third World nationals, or nationalities living in remote areas of the world. I believe everyone is given an opportunity in their lives to hear the claims of Christ. During the years of the first century church, the missionaries could have gone east toward China rather than west toward Europe. But even the Chinese have heard of Jesus Christ. They have ancient writings that told of His coming 2000 years before His birth. Everyone has a choice!

Are you doing everything you can do to provide others with that choice? Jesus Christ left the church in charge of converting the non-believer. Everyone who lives in sin is an evidence of the failure of the church to do the job Christ gave us to do.

## ABOMINABLE

The term abominable is a word I hear old timers using from time to time. What they usually do is get red in the face and put on their church voice and say "this or that is an abomination before God!" The last thing I heard an abomination is

➢ New people in the church talking in the sanctuary before worship.

➢ Drinking coffee in Sunday school.

➢ The Pastor mowing his lawn in his cut-offs.

You can tell from my tone that I am making fun. **We have become too pious and indignant for our own good.** We have missed the whole essence of what abominable is. The word means "to disgust." The root meaning of the original word has a great English vernacular for this word. It means to be inconsistent. An inconsistent life is what being abominable is all about.

The Bible is a book that presents story after story of heroes. Heroes stood steady and strong. Above all else, they were consistent.

Consistency is such a subjective thing. I have heard inconsistent people preach and expound on the life of consistency. It seems we cannot be objective when it comes to ourselves. The only way to personally examine our own life in these terms is to examine the fruit or result of our life.

Several years ago I was driving by one of the busiest intersections in town at Christmas. The traffic was way backed up and it took 10 minutes to get through a light. While waiting, a computerized bank sign caught my eye. It said in a flashing message – SAVINGS — IT DOESN'T MATTER HOW MUCH — BUT HOW OFTEN! The message really stuck with me. I checked a calculator that did a table of savings plans. If a person would invest $30 per week for 35 years they would be a millionaire.

The other day at the mall I got on a computerized scale that cost me a quarter. Not only did this scale tell me how much I weighed, it told me how many calories I should take in for so many days. It was unbelievable. It was like no diet at all.

It was something like 2800 calories per day for 120 days. It all had to do with consistency.

Consistency is easy, as long as we take it a little at a time. It does require staying steady everyday. No splurging is allowed.

Inconsistency is abominable to God. He is raising and nurturing us to be strong and steady — fleeing the up and down spiritual life.

## MURDERERS

This word is easier to interpret than to apply. It is easy to see in the life of the cold-blooded killer. I have met people who were murderers. They are different. It changes someone when they take the life of another. Murder in the original text is "phoneus" which means intentional murder. This is not an accidental killing or a self-defense.

**One kind of murder is abortion.** The killing of unborn children may be legal, but it is murder. Scripturally, the soul is in the body at the point of conception. Whether it is legal or not, it is still murder. An abortion is a killing for convenience. They are performed because a woman can legally have the right to an abortion since January 21, 1973. In *Roe v. Wade,* the Supreme Court determined the termination of pregnancy had to do with the right of privacy. In their line of thought, it is not murder. Unless true repentance and salvation comes to young ladies, many of these people will spend eternity in the lake of fire because of a murdering spirit. All the babies they killed are in heaven today. Their own mother murdered them.

**Another kind of murder is hate.** Jesus introduced this teaching in the Sermon on the Mount. He said that if you have hate thoughts toward someone else you have already murdered them.

# WHOREMONGERS

This is an interesting concept. It has always been interpreted as a sexual term. It is not necessarily a sexual term in the primary sense. The original word "pornos," the way it is used here means to sell for a profit. There is often sexual activity involved, but it is not the initial concept.

The concept is more than just prostitution. It can mean sex for profit, but it happens a lot. Anytime sex is used for promotional reasons or mental dependency, the concept has been brought into play.

It most certainly means pornographic magazines and movies. We need to consider different forms of it as well. Several years ago a couple of men in my church worked for the same employer. This employer was known to give very generous Christmas bonuses. He would throw a big party and give out the checks individually. One of the requirements to receive the check was to allow the boss to give a big wet kiss on the lips to each man's wife. Every man and his wife hated it all, but they put up with it to get their Christmas check. I couldn't believe it. These people stood in line for their checks, putting their wives through embarrassment just to get money. As graphic as it sounds — this is sex for profit!

Another time a man in my church was getting physical with women. He would hug them too hard or touch them in ways that should be only reserved for a husband and wife. These ladies came to me and told me of their predicament. They claimed they didn't like it, but they didn't want to cause trouble. They hadn't said anything to their husbands for fear their husbands would hurt this jerk. I was amazed these women let him get by with this. I often said, "Unless you tell your husbands, you must like it." This deeply offended several of the ladies. They still let him get by with it. This is a form of whoremongering — both on the part of the man and on the part of the ladies. They should have scolded or slapped him.    Letting him get by with it was a sexual profitability to avoid confrontation.

Sex for profit can even happen in marriage.  This is an all too common marital dysfunction.  Don't let this be you.  The idea of being a whoremonger sounds so distasteful but it is grossly common.  Wives put up with abuse, beating, and violence because of money and support.  This is plainly and simply an example of the whoremongering spirit.  If this is you or someone you know, find help through Jesus Christ, counseling, and marital therapy.

## SORCERY

Another citizen of hell is one with the spirit of sorcery. Sorcery comes from the original word "pharmakeus," which refers to a "drug" or a druggist.  In this context, sorcery describes anything that alters the mood or the mind.

For many years I have watched people alter themselves through legal and illegal drugs and controlled substances. Some of these people knew it was wrong.  Others didn't see or hear the harm of their drug activity.  A person who is on drugs or addicted to them finds it hard to communicate about their problem.    Many  recovery  programs  have  been developed  to  help  with  confrontation,  intervention,  and recovery for persons with drug-related problems.

I don't want to knock the medications people use to sustain their lives.  We need to keep a perspective on this.   A balance is important but we must understand that any drug that alters the mind can affect the soul.  It is sorcery.

For God to work in our lives we must be of sound mind.  It is impossible for God to get through to us if our mind is altered.  There is a lot of help for people who want it. The best programs I have seen start with a relationship with God through Jesus Christ. The first thing that has to happen is for the person with a problem to realize there is a problem.

## IDOLATRY

Idols have been mentioned several times in this study. Idol in this text comes from "eidololaties" which means "an image."

An idol is anything that you think more of than God. Anything that gets in between you and your relationship with God is an idol. This is a personal issue which each of us must examine within ourselves.

There are some tie-ins from the original word, which are very important. One tie-in is that what others say or think can be consuming idolatry. The word peer pressure is used to describe those who seek to please or go along with the crowd. This concept infers that those who are consumed with pleasing others are committing this idolatry.

Another tie-in is people worship. Exalting others is idolatry. An extension of this is self-exaltation.

Self-worship is as old as the original sin in the Garden of Eden. Self-worship is the sum total of self-exaltation. People who have not died to the old self will end up in the lake of fire. Self-exaltation is the essence of all other forms of idolatry.

## LIARS

The final citizen of hell mentioned in the text is the liar. The original word "pseudes" means an untruth or an attempt to deceive by falsehood.

There is much deception today. The Bible itself presents many examples of deception. It is also the trick of the serpent on Eve in the Garden of Eden. Watching out for deception can be a full-time job today. We must also guard ourselves against deceiving one another. Telling a lie is only a part of it. Being misleading, telling half-truths, or being deceptive are all things that can creep into our lives.

Maybe you have noticed traces of these eight things in your life. There may be a chance that your life is controlled by one or more of these eight spirits. Not trying to sound too preachy, simple deliverance is possible and available.

# CHAPTER 15

## "HELL YES!"

Being from Iowa and now living in a city, I miss the harvest season. The harvest was always a lot of work. There was always a sense of expectation in the air. It was different if there was a drought or some other natural crisis. In that case, there was a negative feeling in the air.

Jesus used many different illustrations in His teachings. In the great majority of His teaching, he developed an agricultural scenario. Many say it was because Jesus was mostly small town and agricultural. Others say it was to better communicate his deep theological truths to common people. I have always thought Jesus used agricultural illustrations to communicate principles of creation seen in His kingdom.

Matthew chapter 13 gives us the prototype look at the end of time from the teachings of Jesus. It is a vintage agricultural example of a harvest. A careful look at it brings a very graphic picture of God's interest in the human race. This illustration of harvest should open our eyes to some real concerns of God. It should also serve to give us a model of what God expects of us. He is going to hold us accountable for what He expects. This is one of those passages that cannot be overlooked. We must take this scenario head on. Making application of it will make a big difference in our lives and the life to come.

*"Let both grow together until the harvest. At that time I will tell the harvesters: 'First collect the weeds and tie them in bundles to be burned; then gather the wheat and bring it into my barn.' He told them another parable: 'The kingdom of heaven is like a mustard seed, which a man took and planted in his field. Though it is the smallest of all your seeds, yet when it*

*grows, it is the largest of garden plants and becomes a tree, so that the birds of the air come and perch in its branches.' He told them still another parable: 'The kingdom of heaven is like yeast that a woman took and mixed into a large amount of flour until it worked all through the dough.' Jesus spoke all these things to the crowd in parables; he did not say anything to them without using a parable. So was fulfilled what was spoken through the prophet: 'I will open my mouth in parables, I will utter things hidden since the creation of the world.' Then he left the crowd and went into the house. His disciples came to him and said, 'Explain to us the parable of the weeds in the field.' He answered, 'The one who sowed the good seed is the Son of Man. The field is the world, and the good seed stands for the sons of the kingdom. The weeds are the sons of the evil one, and the enemy who sows them is the devil. The harvest is the end of the age, and the harvesters are angels. As the weeds are pulled up and burned in the fire, so it will be at the end of the age. The Son of Man will send out his angels, and they will weed out of his kingdom everything that causes sin and all who do evil. They will throw them into the fiery furnace, where there will be weeping and gnashing of teeth. Then the righteous will shine like the sun in the kingdom of their Father. He who has ears, let him hear. The kingdom of heaven is like treasure hidden in a field. When a man found it, he hid it again, and then in his joy went and sold all he had and bought that field. Again, the kingdom of heaven is like a merchant looking for fine pearls. When he found one of great value, he went away and sold everything he had and bought it. Once again, the kingdom of heaven is like a net that was let down into the lake and caught all kinds of fish. When it was full, the fishermen pulled it up on the shore. Then they sat down and collected the good fish in baskets, but threw the bad away. This is how it will be at the end of the age. The angels will come and separate the wicked from the righteous and throw them into the fiery furnace, where there will be weeping and gnashing of teeth."* — *Matthew 13:30-50*

**The wheat and the tares grow together.**

According to this Scriptural illustration, the wheat is the child of God and the tare is the unredeemed. It is hard to depict the true meaning of what the wheat and the tare would look like. The wheat is the good seed of grain from which so many grain and bran foods are made. A tare is the original Greek word – zizaion — and it means a false grain. A tare could look much like good grain, but it is really poisonous. The wheat and tare grow so close together that one cannot tell the difference from the wheat and the tare.

The tares have a habit of choking out the wheat. It is very important that the good seed get enough sun, rain, and nutrients from the ground. The tares have a tendency to rob the sunlight, and drink the water. They also rob the soil. Somehow through this process, the wheat is forced to either grow stronger or be choked out and die.

So many Christians experience this in their lives. Some feel it in their homes if believers and non-believers live under the same roof. The constant pressure seems insurmountable sometimes. We must realize that the wheat and tares grow together until God says it is time for the harvest. Wheat and tares sometimes grow together at work, in neighborhoods, or in extended family environments. No matter where wheat and tares grow together, it is never easy. The wheat will always feel the presence of the pressure. As wheat, the Christian should always endure the pressure and realize God's purpose is to increase the strength of the wheat.

**The harvest guarantees a crop.**

Not long ago I talked at length with a young man in his 30's who was raising a family. Members of his family were lifelong members of our church. He was raised in the church, but the first chance he had, he quit going to church. Our conversation included talk of all those his age who no longer went to church. This theme seemed to be one which be had expounded many times before. He went on to say that church was totally irrelevant in life. To him, it was all a scam to give preachers a free lunch and living. He continued by saying that in a few years there would be no need for churches since no one his age or younger would even be interested because they understood the scam.

The real truth is, this young man could not have been further from the truth. In an effort to substantiate his misled philosophy, he didn't bother to find out that the church I pastored had tripled in three years. The ballpark we built has 20 teams of young people his age playing on it every week. His futile opinion was that of a tare trying to choke the wheat. Tares justify their behavior and try to convince us there is no wheat at all — and hence no need for a harvest. But there will be a harvest! There is a crop of wheat. Don't let anyone mislead or distract you from being the strong crop of wheat God wants to harvest.

**The wheat is safely protected.**

God allows the wheat to undergo pressure. The reason for this is to strengthen and toughen it. When it comes to the harvest, the wheat will be stored safely in the barn. From the position the text takes, it appears that a harvest like this will never take place again. When the wheat is in the barn it is protected completely.

As wheat, every Christian should become absorbed in the protecting power of God. Each should develop a worldview of the hedge God builds around us.

I remember the testimony of a fellow college student given during a chapel service. It seems she worked in a card shop. One Saturday morning during broad daylight a man with a ski mask over his head and carrying a gun came into the card shop and declared he was there to rob them. This young woman who was newly married was the only one in the card shop. She gave the robber all the cash, but he still jumped over the counter and pushed her down. Terror seized her. Her worst nightmare was about to happen. He ripped her clothes and started to pull down his pants. Suddenly he screamed as if in pain and ran out of the store. Her husband rushed to her side. Later he remarked to her that even Satan had to get God's permission to touch Job. What a powerful thought! We are part of a protected crop of wheat.

The first step to this kind of protection is by being a Christian believer and living in the center of God's will. God's will? This is an important thing that is often dealt with in times of decision. Colleges, marriage, homes, cars — we all have things to decide. We all desperately want to verify God's will in our lives. These critical times should not be the only times we want God's will. Far too long we have made finding God's will a bigger thing than it is. It is true God has a wonderful plan for our lives. God's will is found by following, synthesizing, and applying his Word, the Bible, to our life. By doing this, the believer, as wheat, will always be protected.

**The energy from the furnace comes from the tares as they burn.**

Any dry, dead stock of grain burns fast and hot. The idea of "furnace" in Matthew 13 is a fire that is burning hot and hasn't yet reached its height of consumption. This picture of the furnace of fire and agriculture is from Jesus' own teaching. It is the same fire seen in Revelation chapter 21. Jesus gives us a different vantage point. This one is the parallel between wheat and the Christian and the sinner and tare. The real clincher is the paradox of the burning of the tares and the safety of the wheat in the barn.

# CHAPTER 16

## "A HELL OF A CHOICE"

The battle of all time is the battle of wills — ours against God. God is trying to fill that empty void in our spirit. It is God's will that all men come to him.

**The plan of God is free will.**

*"Where were you when I laid the earth's foundation? Tell me, if you understand. Who marked off its dimensions? Surely you know! Who stretched a measuring line across it? On what were its footings set, or who laid its cornerstone — while the morning stars sang together and all the angels shouted for joy?"* — *Job 38:4-7*

The scene is set. Ions of time ago God laid the foundation of the world. Out of Him came creation. How? Only God knows. Why? Fellowship between us. God yearns to share Himself — to give Himself away. This type of giving love is part of God's being.

As Job questioned God — God came back with a reply. Job didn't have enough wisdom to sit in judgment of God's decisions. The reply is very clear that the world was in harmony with itself. The morning stars sang together. This is a reference to angels. Angels are higher than man. They have greater intelligence and more power than man does. They have a personal audience with God. These beings shouted with joy at God's demonstration of power. There was not any fighting, or arguing about position in God's kingdom. It is clear that at this point of creation, no rebellion had taken place.

Lucifer held the highest, most exalted position in the spirit realm. Lucifer was the most beautiful, rich, and intellectual of all God's creation. He was perfect in every way.

As God created, He didn't want puppets. He didn't want robots. He didn't want dupes. He wanted a creation that chose to serve him because it wanted to — not because it was forced to, but because it chose to do so from a free will.

> *"The word of the LORD came to me: Son of man, take up a lament concerning the king of Tyre and say to him: 'This is what the Sovereign LORD says: You were the model of perfection, full of wisdom and perfect in beauty. You were in Eden, the garden of God; every precious stone adorned you: ruby, topaz and emerald, chrysolite, onyx and jasper, sapphire, turquoise and beryl. Your settings and mountings were made of gold; on the day you were created they were prepared. You were anointed as a guardian cherub, for so I ordained you. You were on the holy mount of God; you walked among the fiery stones. You were blameless in your ways from the day you were created till wickedness was found in you'"* — Ezekiel 28:11-15

The King of Tyre, as we see in this passage, is that one creation of God, the highest of all God's creation: Lucifer. Lucifer held the highest, most exalted position in all of God's creation.

Look at the description of Lucifer:

> ➢ Full of wisdom and perfection in beauty. The most beautiful and wise of all of God's creation.

> ➢ The anointed cherub who covers. A cherub is of high rank. They are linked to God's holy presence and glory. God can find the irony of Lucifer in a cherub proclaimed righteous. Lucifer, instead, began to proclaim his own righteousness.

- ➤ Anointed. In other words, someone who leads.

- ➤ All the jewels go further to show his rank.

- ➤ Eden. Holy mountain of God. In the midst of the stones of fire. All show his relationship to God.

This passage is speaking of the greatest being that God ever created. Yet Lucifer was no robot. He had a will of his own. He chose to glorify God himself. That is the kind of God we serve. He gives us a choice. God's plan is in free will. Those who follow him choose to do so. The objective of this free will he offers us is to have a functioning, thinking creation with an intellect that can serve Him because he wants to. The earth was provided for us to build us, grow us, and purge us. Tests and trials come only to make us strong. Somewhere in another dimension we shall see why all the pain and why all the problems. Right now, free will is really our freedom —or our bondage.

We have the capacity to make our own decisions in our daily lives. How much better it would be to ask ourselves the question — How will this affect my eternal life? By some unknown reason, everything that happens in this life is tied to the next life. For this reason we must watch free will closely. God keeps careful track of Lucifer as recorded in Isaiah 14:12-14 —the process of Lucifer's will, the free will he was given to serve God perfectly, or in his case, to exercise it against God to serve himself. What happened when Lucifer fell? The answer is found in the following passage:

*"In the beginning God created the heavens and the earth. Now the earth was formless and empty, darkness was over the surface of the deep, and the Spirit of God was hovering over the waters." — Genesis 1:1-2*

*"So God created man in his own image, in the image of God he created him; male and female he created them."* — Genesis 1:27

*"Can both fresh water and salt water flow from the same spring?"* — James 3:11

At the time of the fall of Lucifer, God had dual dimensions. One was heaven; the other was earth. It must have been possible to descend and ascend them. There was a glorious purpose for existence. When Lucifer's will became contrary to God's will, chaos developed. That is why we see in verse one that the earth was without form and void. This means chaotic in the Hebrew. The earth became dark from sin. God then had to produce a laboratory to fulfill His purpose. He needed to produce a race to end this rebellion — end it by gaining victory. The earth was cleared. A new dimension was prepared for Lucifer and those who follow him:

*"Then he will say to those on his left, 'Depart from me, you who are cursed, into the eternal fire prepared for the devil and his angels.'"* — Matthew 25:41

The earth is the battlefield between good and evil. Mankind is the laboratory rat. If man can gain victory over his own will, he can become greater in position than even God's angels. The earth is under a magnifying glass, the host of heaven watch. A play to beat all plays is played out every day. The destiny of all things hangs in the balance all because God wants people to serve Him because they want to.

**The basis of sin is "I will."**

*"How you have fallen from heaven, O morning star, son of the dawn! You have been cast down to the earth, you that once laid low the nations! You said in your heart, 'I will ascend to heaven; I will raise my throne*

162

*above the stars of God; I will sit enthroned on the mount of assembly, on the utmost heights of the sacred mountain. I will ascend above the tops of the clouds; I will make myself like the Most High."* — *Isaiah 14:12-14*

From the previous passage, we see that Lucifer was perfect until unrighteousness was found in him, which unrighteousness was his own selfish will. Further, this selfish will was contrary to God's will. This is the basis of sin — my will contradicting God's will. Five times Lucifer says, "**I will**." The passage says that Lucifer said it in his heart. That is where sin originates. Our hearts can harden or soften. It takes a great softening to come to God. It also takes a hardening for us to turn our backs on Him.

How can I know God's will? This is a common question often asked. What did God provide to reveal his will?

> ➤ **Jesus Christ.** God came in the flesh to provide a way of overcoming our will. God wanted to show all creation the extent of his love. What did he show? There was no extent to his love — the creator dying for His creation. The thought of it paralyzes all the realm of evil. It is so contrary to Lucifer. God died to all of His self will to show that self will has no place in God.

> ➤ **The Bible.** The truths of God's word reveal His will.

> ➤ **Ask.** "*If any of you lacks wisdom, he should ask God, who gives generously to all without finding fault, and it will be given to him. But when he asks, he must believe and not doubt, because he who doubts is like a wave of the sea, blown and tossed by the wind.*" — James 1:5-6

> ➤ **Pray.** Pray that His desires become your desires.

➢ **Trust.** Trust that directs you.

The basis of sin is: **"I will."**

## God accepts whosoever will.

God accepts who ever gives up **"I will."** This is not just a play on words. We have a free will and the earth is the laboratory. God makes Himself available to people personally. His will is that we all follow it.

# CHAPTER 17

# " TO HELL WITH THE DEVIL!"

*"And the angels who did not keep their positions of authority but abandoned their own home — these he has kept in darkness, bound with everlasting chains for judgment on the great Day."   — Jude 1:6*

*"Snatch others from the fire and save them; to others show mercy, mixed with fear — hating even the clothing stained by corrupted flesh."   — Jude 1:23*

*"The fifth angel sounded his trumpet, and I saw a star that had fallen from the sky to the earth. The star was given the key to the shaft of the Abyss. When he opened the Abyss, smoke rose from it like the smoke from a gigantic furnace. The sun and sky were darkened by the smoke from the Abyss."   — Revelation 9:1-2*

*"He, too, will drink of the wine of God's fury, which has been poured full strength into the cup of his wrath. He will be tormented with burning sulfur in the presence of the holy angels and of the Lamb. And the smoke of their torment rises for ever and ever. There is no rest day or night for those who worship the beast and his image, or for anyone who receives the mark of his name."   — Revelation 14:10-11*

*"But the beast was captured, and with him the false prophet who had performed the miraculous signs on his behalf. With these signs he had deluded those who had received the mark of the beast and worshiped his image. The two of them were thrown alive into the fiery lake of burning sulfur."   — Revelation 19:20*

*"And the devil, who deceived them, was thrown into the lake of burning sulfur, where the beast and the false prophet had been thrown. They will be tormented*

*day and night for ever and ever." — Revelation 20:10*

*"If anyone's name was not found written in the book of life, he was thrown into the lake of fire." — Revelation 20:15*

Through the years I have been a Christian, I have probably heard just about every possible opinion about the devil. Some believe the devil is so powerful and brutal he could squash the Christians of this world like a bug. Others believe the opposite —the Christian believer has all the power over Satan. Then there are many variations in between.

The proper view is more of a mentality than it is an opinion. It is a way of life rather than a state of mind. This way of life has the same format as all the other models we have developed throughout this study on hell. The realm of evil is a positive one. It is positive only because it has a positive purpose and that is to rid the world of evil through creating an environment whereby people choose whom they will serve.

In the last chapter we looked at the freedom of choice. By having the freedom of choice, people become either stronger or weaker in their faith — stronger if they resist evil, and weaker if they submit to temptation. James says that if you resist the devil, He will flee from you. The idea of resist is the ability to stand in contrast. In this way, we see that the study of hell can be a very positive experience. By studying Scripture we are able to find out everything we need to know about the devil, hell, and the realm of evil. Through this knowledge, we will have everything at our disposal to stand in contrast to him, resist, and thereby have him flee from us!

Recently, I was watching a Christian television station, when a guest preacher came on. He is quite well known in some areas of the country. The first words out of his mouth were: "Ta hell with the devil!" The studio audience had obviously heard him do this before and they all repeated together — "Ta hell with the devil."

When I first got started in full-time ministry, I was a youth pastor. The church was large enough, but had just hired a full-time Christian education director. I worked under him, taking care of details and running the senior high youth program. One of the things I did was pick up teens needing a ride to church on Wednesday night. A boy in a wheelchair was on my run, and also in my youth group. He lived in a state-operated nursing home for abandoned and handicapped children. He was born with an open spine. His mother left him on the steps of the welfare department at his birth. He was an extremely odd person. He had as many emotional handicaps as he did physical handicaps. Guy and I developed a pretty good relationship. Whenever he got on the nerves of the church people, they would come to me and I would have a talk with him. It seemed like I toted him everywhere. He was under state care, so whenever I took him out, I had to go through all the red tape of documenting and verification. I even became bonded to do so.

Guy had no concept of family life and would develop crushes on married women. He would call them and ask them out on dates. I would get a call from an infuriated husband and have to immediately go over to the children's home and talk to him.

Shortly after he turned 18, the state developed a program to let these young people move out and live partly on their own in little apartments. The day he moved out, he never wanted to go to church again. I made repeated attempts to go to his apartment, but no one ever seemed to be at home. Finally, in a desperate attempt to make contact, I hung out at his door, waiting for him to come home. After about 10 minutes of waiting, I heard the television go on inside. It dawned on me that Guy was just not answering his door. "Guy," I yelled.

"Go away," he yelled back.

"Open the door!" I insisted.

He cracked the door a little.

"I don't want to have anything to do with you, and I have nothing to say to you. Go away, and don't come back," he said.

At this point I put my foot in the door. At the same time he slammed the door, but to no avail.

"Guy, what has happened?" I inquired.

"If you don't move your foot, I will call the police."

"I don't understand Guy. What has happened between us?"

Then he said it. With no reason, he hit me with the ultimate curse of rejection: **"You can go straight to hell!"**

Those were his last words to me. I had never been told that from someone I had done so much for. I had poured my life into the guy. What had I done wrong?

The biggest lesson I learned was just how it must make God feel to be let down by us. In just a very small measure I felt something like that. God has provided everything we need for joy in this life and the one to come, and yet we tell Him to go to hell by our own apathy. Another lesson I learned is just how active the devil is today. He is the one I want to tell, **"to hell with the devil**." I join in with that television preacher I watched that day.

The truth is, the lake of fire is exactly his destiny. God has prepared the lake of fire for him and he knows it. His whole purpose is to mask, deceive, destroy, sift, and devour.

Whatever it takes, the devil desires to take as many people with him as possible.

Have you ever wanted to say, **"to hell with the devil"**? There is a way to do it. It is through living a positive lifestyle and reminding the devil of his destiny.

I have a friend who is a theological liberal. He doesn't believe in a literal Satan. He says we blame Satan for many things that are our own doing. He has a point, but in thought he is wrong. Satan is real.

There are two things we can do to say, **"to hell with the devil."** These two things are godly discipline and God centered initiative.

## GODLY DISCIPLINE

Discipline is the key to the God-centered, consistent Christian life. Most of the time when we think of discipline, we think of children.

*"Do not withhold discipline from a child; if you punish him with the rod, he will not die. Punish him with the rod and save his soul from death."* — Proverbs 23:13-14

With child abuse so prevalent today, we need to be careful of the type of discipline, but indeed, discipline clearly provides a way of deliverance from hell's way. The logic is simple — discipline makes it easier for us to create boundaries and limits for ourselves. In the early stages of a child's life, he needs limits and boundaries set for him and then enforced. As a child grows and matures, the sense of discipline needs to be continued to bring out a sense of self-discipline. Finally, in adulthood, discipline creates a way of life that directs itself toward God — consistency, faithfulness, and overcoming erratic behavior.

In the same way, God is our heavenly Father and seeks to develop a deeply spiritual sense of discipline with the child of God. God seeks to have a growing, dynamic and intimate relationship with every Christian. The way of Christ is the way of discipline.

Discipline is the ability to be moderate in all things. Scripture demands this of us. The inability to be moderate in all things creates an atmosphere of imbalance.

People who take things to an extreme have moderation problems. The person with an addictive personality has acute moderation problems and yet discipline is the thing they need the most. A disciplined life is the only salvation that one can have.

Discipline also provides accountability. Accountability is tough because it can be embarrassing. It is very important because accountability helps provide boundaries.

Accountability is a deeply personal thing. We need to set up our own system of accountability with trusted friends, loved ones, or counselors.

## GOD CENTERED INITIATIVE

The second way we say **"to hell with the devil"** is through our own initiative and applications of what God is teaching us. One of the biggest problems I find Christians have in their spiritual lives is in the area of their reactions to things. Most Christians feel bad or guilty because they feel that their reactions are not very Christ-like. The truth is, God does not want the Christian believer to react, but instead to act!

**Action!** Initiative to glorify God is the whole purpose of the church. Jesus proclaimed this truth in the Sermon on the Mount. He told us that we are the salt of the earth and the light of the world. These statements of Jesus are divine appointments to lead the way and forge the direction for the world to follow. Matthew, chapter 25 gives us the meat.

> *"Take the talent from him and give it to the one who has the ten talents. For everyone who has will be given more, and he will have an abundance. Whoever does not have, even what he has will be taken from him. And throw that worthless servant outside, into the darkness, where there will be weeping and gnashing of teeth."*
> — *Matthew 25:28-30*

> *"Then he will say to those on his left, 'Depart from me, you who are cursed, into the eternal fire prepared for the devil and his angels."* — *Matthew 25:41*

> *"Then they will go away to eternal punishment, but the righteous to eternal life."* — *Matthew 25:46*

The reason that man is unprofitable is because he buried his talents out of fear that he would lose what he had. His worst fear came to pass. He lost a lot more than his talents, he lost his soul. The unprofitable servant reacted rather than acted.

We must extend this scenario into our everyday lives. God would rather us act and lose than to react and do nothing. His will is for the body of Christ to lead the way. The way we lead is to get out in the trenches. Be someone on the front line for Jesus.

Recently I received a letter from a traveling gospel group. I am a member of their board of directors. The manager of the group said, "Well, we sure have given the devil a black eye!" He was talking about all the people getting saved during their concerts. His phrase is one commonly used in some church circles. Other church circles feel it is silly to depict the devil with a black eye. Either way, we need to show initiative by acting rather then reacting!

# "MAD AS HELL"

## A Conclusion

I wonder how many of you made it all the way through this! Through my study, writing, and praying something has changed within me. I feel kind of sorry for my church people who first heard this material during preaching. After each sermon, I gave a strong altar call. I got into it so strongly I felt like the persona of the old time preacher — red faced, loud voice, collar unbuttoned, and jacket off.

Through this study I have reached some personal conclusions which I want to share. I hope they are adaptable to you and your life.

**I conclude that there is pain much like hell in this world. This pain can be both emotional and physical. This pain is used by God to strengthen the soul to avoid eternal hell.**

> *"The cords of death entangled me, the anguish of the grave came upon me; I was overcome by trouble and sorrow."* — *Psalms 116:3*

**I conclude that hell serves a great redeeming purpose, and is therefore a positive force in God's redemption process.**

> *"But God will redeem my life from the grave; he will surely take me to himself."* — *Psalms 49:15*

The whole idea people bring up that a loving God would not send a person to hell is right. A loving God is only loving if He is righteous. Righteousness has as its core the redemptive acts of bringing about righteousness. God makes righteousness manifest by providing a Savior to redeem. In this act of redemption, those who do not serve Jesus send themselves to hell.

I conclude that many people accept Christ as savior just to avoid hell — we should challenge these people to deepen their faith so that they serve God, not to avoid hell, but because they love Him.

*"And I — in righteousness I will see your face; when I awake, I will be satisfied with seeing your likeness."* — *Psalms 17:15*

I conclude that we should never back down from our proclamation that there is a hell to avoid, no matter what others may say.

It is God's will that no one perish. We must do everything in our power to help others avoid hell. All we have is what is present before us to share Christ. Tomorrow may be too late for many.

*"It is not the dead who praise the LORD, those who go down to silence;"* — *Psalms 115:17*

I conclude that any sacrifice in this life is worth it to avoid the lake of fire.

Whatever is required to make heaven is worth it. Any discomfort is strictly momentary.

### AND FINALLY

I have called these concluding remarks "as mad as hell!" My greatest concern for the church today is there are too few people truly prepared to help others avoid hell.